by
Bob Umlas

T0206657

Holy Macro! Books
PO Box 541731
Merritt Island, FL 32954

Cool Excel Sh*t

Printed in the USA by Hess Print Solutions

First Printing: April 2022 (e-book April 2021)

Author: Bob Umlas

Cover Design: Shannon Travise

Publisher: Bill Jelen

Index: Nellie Jay

Tech Editor: Bill Jelen

Published by Holy Macro! Books, PO Box 541731, Merritt Island FL 32954

Distributed by Independent Publishers Group, Chicago IL

ISBN 978-1-61547-073-0 (print) 978-1-61547-159-1 (digital)

Library of Congress Control Number: 2021TBD

Table of Contents

VBA

Other books by Bob Umlas:
This isn't Excel, it's Magic (2005)
This isn't Excel, it's Magic 2nd Edition (2007)
Excel Outside the Box (2012)
More Excel Outside the Box (2015)
Excel Preschool (2019)

Foreword

I actually learned Microsoft Excel on the Macintosh in 1986 or so, using version 0.99! When the real version (1.00?) shipped, I read the manual (yes, Excel came with manuals then) from cover to cover. Six times. Especially in order to learn Data Tables. I just didn't get it. (Okay, so I'm a geek. Actually, I once heard that you're a geek if you double-click the TV remote)!

Around 1993 I received the nickname "Excel Trickster" from one Will Tompkins, a real Excel Guru. I got that because during a seminar he was hosting in Washington, I believe, for what he called the Excel SWAT team, he was showing his then famous Tompkins methodology – a macro structure using Excel 4 style macros (before VBA existed in Excel) which was quite sophisticated. He showed a line of code which used a range name, a label, and he wanted to show us the code at that label. So, he used F5(Goto), and we saw literally many hundreds of defined names which he had to laboriously scroll through to get to the one he was looking for. After he had done this about 4-5 times, I raised my hand and said, "You know, you can get to that label directly. Just press Ctrl/[." He tried it and was flabbergasted! So, he tried it again. Then he remarked that I just saved him about 2 hours every day scrolling through his defined names!

When I also told him you could *return* to the location you were just at by using Ctrl/], he called me the Excel Trickster, and that nickname has stuck with me ever since. So, thank you, Will.

I've been an Excel MVP for 25 years – 1993-2018, and I currently lead an online Master Class in Excel which is 12 3-hour sessions and a VBA class which is 2 3-hour sessions. I have presented at various global events (EIEFreshTalk and GlobalExcelSummit) with 1750 and 9400+ participants, respectively!

Acknowledgments

I'd like to thank my wife, Judy, for her continued support of my pursuing my Excel "studies", former and current Excel MVPs for their continued eye-opening ideas upon which I have built some of these ideas.

Several ideas in this book were first discussed in the 2007 book, "This Isn't Excel, It's Magic", published by IIL Publishing in New York. That book features 111 Excel tips and is still available from the publisher.

FORMULAS

An amazing formula to SUMIF the visible rows
This isn't so much a tip/trick (it's a bit advanced), but worth visiting!

Let's look at a worksheet containing the source data:

	A	B	C
1	Service	City	Amount
2	JKP	New York	3112
3	ES	New York	2475
4	AW	Miami	2018
5	AW	Atlanta	9893
6	BU	Amsterdam	328
7	ES	Atlanta	597
8	BU	Atlanta	2607
9	NNR	Boston	5278
10	NNR	Amsterdam	1836
11	BU	San Francisco	73
12	JKP	Miami	2667
13	ES	New York	4215

And let's say this goes down to row 123. I inserted a slicer for this data:

City

- Amsterdam
- Atlanta
- Boston
- Los Angeles
- Miami
- New York
- Redmond
- San Francisco

…then I cut this slicer and pasted it to another sheet:

	A	B	C	E	F
1	**Subtotal 109:**	592763	**City**		
2		**#VALUE!**	Amsterdam		
3					
4	**Service**	**Total**	Atlanta		
5	ES	131174	Boston		
6	BU	96757	Los Angeles		
7	AW	129093	Miami		
8	NNR	129979			
9	JKP	105760	New York		
10			Redmond		
11	**Total**	592763	San Francisco		
12					

It's fairly straightforward to get the right formula in cell B1 to add up all the values from the source sheet, depending on the choices in the slicer:

=SUBTOTAL(109,'Supporting Data'!C:C)

This is because the choices in the slicer will hide/show the appropriate rows and the SUBTOTAL(109,… will summarize the unhidden rows.

But how can you further break it down by service so the numbers in B5:B9 can be determined? The #VALUE! Error in B2 is a first attempt. We need to pretty much use the same SUBTOTAL formula as in B1, but perhaps pass this to a SUMPRODUCT formula: =SUMPRODUCT(SUBTOTAL(109,'Supporting Data'!C2:C123),N('Supporting Data'!$A$2:$A$123=A5))

This seems like it should work – but it gives that #VALUE! error. Why? It's because the first part (the SUBTOTAL) gives just one value, and the 2nd part gives an array of values:

It becomes =SUMPRODUCT(592763,N('Supporting Data'!$A$2:$A$123=A5)) which becomes =SUMPRODUCT(592763,{0;1;0;0;0;1;0;0;0;0;0;1;0; 0;0;0;0;1; 1;0;1;1;0;0;0;0;0;0;0;0;0;0;1;0;0;0;1;0;0;0;1;0;0;1;0;0;0;0;0;1;0;0;0;0;0;1;0;1;0;1 ;0;0;0;0;0;0;0;0;1;0;0;0;0;0;1;0;0;0;0;0;0;1;0;0;0;1;0;0;0;0;0;0;0;0;0;0;0;0;0;1 ;0;0;0;0;0;0;0;0;0;1;1;0;0;1;0;1;0;0;1;0}) which simply doesn't balance. There needs to be the same number of values in each section. So how do we make this happen? Let's look at the solution and see how it works:

=SUMPRODUCT(SUBTOTAL(109,OFFSET('Supporting Data'!$C$1, SEQUENCE(122),0)),N('Supporting Data'!$A$2:$A$123=A5)) does the job. Let's break this down.

The magic is really in the OFFSET formula:

> =SUMPRODUCT(SUBTOTAL(109,OFFSET('Supporting Data'!$C$1,SEQUENCE(122),0)),N('Supporting Data'!$A$2:$A$123=A5))

This expands to the following:

> =SUMPRODUCT(SUBTOTAL(109,{3112;2475;2018;9893;328;597;2607;5278;1836;73;2667;4215;124;4525;2958;9237;5193;2832;9005;962;2720;
> 5814;3720;523;8947;2300;629;1736;3320;2505;2088;8038;8308;1290;6970;930;6840;6333;5880;7929;9954;7213;8389;9347;6693;9268;7837;
> 177;5690;6379;7858;5010;1756;5424;9641;1788;7939;2905;989;1690;8418;9529;7153;6886;7401;1971;5806;7576;5572;3107;7122;2821;929;
> 7983;7931;2602;9469;4034;6700;8875;1246;4348;8241;5968;2148;700;3208;2931;4179;2959;9383;4785;3499;7652;3020;1578;9700;7849;
> 8188;6959;7813;1197;789;9553;8722;744;4373;6514;2740;2263;3515;4862;5478;4575;1379;8809;8618;1635;1647;295;9157;4957}),N(
> 'Supporting Data'!$A$2:$A$123=A5))

Notice that we now are going to have the same number of values in each argument to the SUMPRODUCT function. The above expands to:

> =SUMPRODUCT(SUBTOTAL(109,{3112;2475;2018;9893;328;597;2607;5278;1836;73;2667;4215;124;4525;2958;9237;5193;2832;9005;962;2720;
> 5814;3720;523;8947;2300;629;1736;3320;2505;2088;8038;8308;1290;6970;930;6840;6333;5880;7929;9954;7213;8389;9347;6693;9268;7837;
> 177;5690;6379;7858;5010;1756;5424;9641;1788;7939;2905;989;1690;8418;9529;7153;6886;7401;1971;5806;7576;5572;3107;7122;2821;929;
> 7983;7931;2602;9469;4034;6700;8875;1246;4348;8241;5968;2148;700;3208;2931;4179;2959;9383;4785;3499;7652;3020;1578;9700;7849;
> 8188;6959;7813;1197;789;9553;8722;744;4373;6514;2740;2263;3515;4862;5478;4575;1379;8809;8618;1635;1647;295;9157;4957}),{0;1;0;0;0;1;
> 0;0;0;0;1;0;0;0;0;0;1;1;0;1;1;0;0;0;0;0;0;0;0;1;0;0;0;1;0;0;0;1;0;0;1;0;0;1;0;0;0;0;1;0;0;0;0;0;1;0;1;0;1;0;0;0;0;0;0;0;0;1;0;0;0;0;0;1;0;0;0;0;0;1;0;
> 0;0;1;0;0;0;0;0;0;0;0;0;0;0;1;0;0;0;0;0;0;0;0;0;1;1;0;0;1;0;1;0;0;0;1;0})

And the result is what we're looking for. SEQUENCE(122) generates values 1,2,3…,122 and the offset from C1 for 1,2,3…122 is C2, C3, C4,…,C123 where C123 is the last cell in the source data. This could also have been OFFSET('Supporting Data'!$C$1,ROW($1:$122),0) using ROW instead of SEQUENCE.

This responds to the slicer settings (the formula in B5 is shown via a FORMULATEXT in H5):

	A	B	C	E	F	G	H
1	Subtotal 109:	156592					
2		#VALUE!					
3							
4	Service	Total	**City**				
			Amsterdam				=SUMPRODUCT(SUBTOTAL(109,OFFSET('Supporting
			Atlanta				Data'!$C$1,SEQUENCE(122),0)),N('Supporting
5	ES	23522	Boston				Data'!$A$2:$A$123=A5))
6	BU	18925					
7	AW	32408	Los Angeles				
8	NNR	39189	Miami				
9	JKP	42548					
10			New York				
11	Total	156592	Redmond				
12			San Francisco				
13							

Putting in a Grand Total of data already subtotaled

Suppose you have a worksheet which looks like this (note that the screen is split and rows 13:127 are not shown):

	A	B	C
1		22	
2		20	
3		15	
4		6	
5		98	
6		94	
7		24	
8		49	
9		47	
10		81	
11	Subtotal	456	
12		29	
128		74	
129		96	
130		55	
131		12	
132		54	
133	Subtotal	540	
134	Grand Total	??	
135			

You want to put the grand total in cell B134. There are many Subtotals, like in cells B11 and B133, and many more which are not shown. And they are =SUM(…) formulas, not =SUBTOTAL(9,…) formulas. (Had they been SUBTO-TAL formulas, then a simple =SUBTOTAL(9,B1:B133) would have worked fine because the SUBTOTAL formula ignores other SUBTOTAL formulas in the reference.) What formula should you use? One possibility is =B133+B120+B100+B76+B62+B47+B24+B11.This works but is subject to clicking the wrong cell(s) when entering it. I've actually seen formulas like this which made the formula bar span 3 rows!

Another is =SUMIF(A1:A133,"Subtotal",B1:B133). This is much better, as it is less error-prone (assuming the word "Subtotal" in column A is in the right rows!)

Another choice is =SUMPRODUCT(N(A1:A133="Subtotal"),B1:B133).This works as well, but the arguments must be numeric. If the formula had been =SUMPRODUCT(A1:A133="Subtotal",B1:B133) – without the N(…), then the result would be zero because the first array would be one of TRUEs and FALSEs, which is not numeric. N(TRUE) is 1, and N(FALSE) is 0, so this works.

Another is pressing Alt/= in cell B134! This has Excel give =SUM(B133,B120, B100,B76,B62,B47,B24,B11) which is less error prone (it finds the other SUM formulas in the range!), but not as fast to calculate as the winner:

=SUM(B1:B133)/2. Wait! How does this work? Well, look at the figure again. B1:B10 total 456, because that's what the formula in B11 says: =SUM(B1:B10). So B1:B10 is 456 and B11 is 456, so the 456 is in there twice! So, divide by 2!!

Using notes inside formulas via the N-function
The N function, shown here:

Insert Function   **?**   **✕**

Search for a function:

| | **Go** |

Or select a *category*: All   ⌄

Select a functio*n*:

MROUND	⌃
MULTINOMIAL	
MUNIT	
N	
NA	
NEGBINOM.DIST	
NEGBINOMDIST	⌄

N(value)
Converts non-number value to a number, dates to serial numbers, TRUE to 1, anything else to 0 (zero).

<u>Help on this function</u>   **OK**   **Cancel**

Converts non-number to a number, dates to serial numbers, True to 1, anything else to 0. Well, you can take advantage of this knowledge inside a formula. For example:

✕ ✓ *fx*	=VLOOKUP(B22,xyztable,3,FALSE)+N("this will search the table for the z-factor")								
D	E	F	G	H	I	J	K	
0.923539								

This formula now explains that the VLOOKUP is searching xyztable's third column for the occurrence of cell B22's value for the z-factor (whatever *that* is). The point being that the part of the formula, N("This will search the table for the z-factor") will be zero, not effecting the result. So, you can use the N-function inside formulas like this to document or comment on a part of the formula by effectively adding 0.

Fun with relatively defined names

If, *while on cell A1*, you define a name, z, to be =!A1:Z100 like shown:

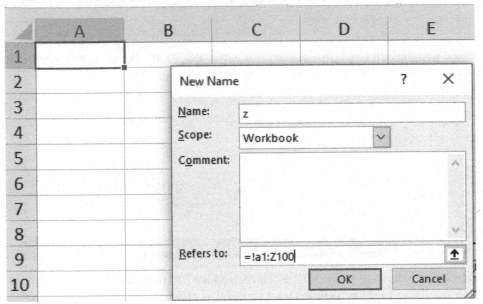

then you can use this name to scroll the active cell to the top left of the work-sheet!

For example, suppose you have a worksheet which looks like this:

	A	B	C	D	E	F	G	H	I	J	K	L	M
1	Product	Year	Quarter	Sales Rep	Region	Units	Sales						
2	Dairy	1997	1	Aguilar	North	5563	20001.98						
3	Produce	1997	1	Johnson	West	1242	19742.51						
4	Produce	1997	1	Johnson	South	983	21501.40						
5	Dairy	1997	2	Johnson	North	3833	20569.94						
6	Dairy	1997	2	Johnson	East	3216	22679.72						
7	Produce	1997	3	Aguilar	South	8160	17827.49						
8	Dairy	1997	3	Aguilar	West	2790	14017.85						
9	Produce	1997	4	Aguilar	East	9265	24625.34						
10	Produce	1997	4	Johnson	North	3868	732.41						
11	Dairy	1997	4	Johnson	West	1773	23300.78						
12	Dairy	1997	4	Aguilar	North	6290	17275.28						
13	Produce	1998	1	Aguilar	West	9888	15810.14						
14	Produce	1998	1	Aguilar	North	39	1648.56						
15	Dairy	1998	1	Aguilar	East	9970	20814.45		Sum of Units	Region	Sales Rep		
16	Dairy	1998	2	Johnson	South	3656	24029.99			East		East Total	North
17	Dairy	1998	2	Johnson	North	2730	3851.90		Product	Aguilar	Johnson		Aguila
18	Dairy	1998	3	Aguilar	South	3670	9747.47		Dairy	9970	3216	13186	118
19	Dairy	1998	3	Aguilar	West	1695	10203.70		Produce	13926	8722	22648	92
20	Dairy	1998	4	Aguilar	West	9550	15860.64		Grand Total	23896	11938	35834	211
21	Produce	1998	4	Johnson	East	8722	22656.52						
22	Produce	1998	4	Aguilar	East	4661	14920.45						
23	Produce	1998	4	Aguilar	North	9213	14056.66						
24													

and you'd like to see more of the pivot table. Certainly, you can scroll both horizontally and vertically, but you can also take advantage of this newly defined name, z. Click on cell I15, then use F5 and goto z. The result will be this:

	I	J	K	L	M	N	O	P	Q	R	S
15	Sum of Units	Region [▼]	Sales Rep [▼]								
16		East		East Total	North		North Total	South		South Total	West
17	Product [▼]	Aguilar	Johnson		Aguilar	Johnson		Aguilar	Johnson		Aguilar J
18	Dairy	9970	3216	13186	11853	6563	18416	3670	3656	7326	14035
19	Produce	13926	8722	22648	9252	3868	13120	8160	1000000	1008160	9888
20	Grand Total	23896	11938	35834	21105	10431	31536	11830	1003656	1015486	23923
21											

Notice that the cell has been scrolled to the top left. That's because, from cell I15, the definition of z is as in this illustration:

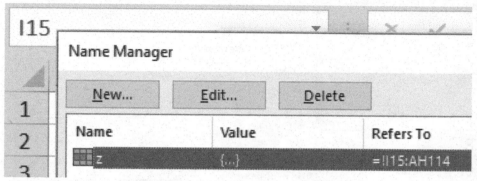

-- a relative reference to the active cell resized by 100 rows and 26 columns. In order for Excel to show as much as it can of this range, it scrolls the worksheet!

Z is defined with a leading exclamation mark so that the sheet name is *not* appended to the name, and you can use z to be a 100x26 shape in any sheet!

Bulk formula change

Suppose you have a worksheet with references to many sheets like this:

A1				fx	'=Sheet2!1:1048576
	A	B	C	D	E
1	=Sheet2!1:1048576				
2	=Sheet3!1:1048576				
3	=Sheet4!1:1048576				
4	=Sheet5!1:1048576				
5	=Sheet6!1:1048576				
6	=Sheet7!1:1048576				
7	=Sheet8!1:1048576				
8	=Sheet9!1:1048576				
9	=Sheet10!1:1048576				
10	=Sheet11!1:1048576				
11	=Sheet12!1:1048576				
12	=Sheet13!1:1048576				
13	=Sheet14!1:1048576				
14	=Sheet15!1:1048576				
15	=Sheet16!1:1048576				

And you want to put in column B these formulas corresponding to what's in column A: =COUNTA(INDIRECT("Sheet2!1:1048576")) in B1 through =COUNTA(INDIRECT("Sheet16!1:1048576")) in B16.

It could be done with a VBA routine, but here's a way to do it with formulas:

Look at the formulas in B here:

B1			fx	="=COUNTA(INDIRECT("""&MID(A1,2,255)&""))"		
	A	B		C	D	E
1	=Sheet2!1:1048576	=COUNTA(INDIRECT("Sheet2!1:1048576"))				
2	=Sheet3!1:1048576	=COUNTA(INDIRECT("Sheet3!1:1048576"))				
3	=Sheet4!1:1048576	=COUNTA(INDIRECT("Sheet4!1:1048576"))				
4	=Sheet5!1:1048576	=COUNTA(INDIRECT("Sheet5!1:1048576"))				
5	=Sheet6!1:1048576	=COUNTA(INDIRECT("Sheet6!1:1048576"))				
6	=Sheet7!1:1048576	=COUNTA(INDIRECT("Sheet7!1:1048576"))				
7	=Sheet8!1:1048576	=COUNTA(INDIRECT("Sheet8!1:1048576"))				
8	=Sheet9!1:1048576	=COUNTA(INDIRECT("Sheet9!1:1048576"))				
9	=Sheet10!1:1048576	=COUNTA(INDIRECT("Sheet10!1:1048576"))				
10	=Sheet11!1:1048576	=COUNTA(INDIRECT("Sheet11!1:1048576"))				
11	=Sheet12!1:1048576	=COUNTA(INDIRECT("Sheet12!1:1048576"))				
12	=Sheet13!1:1048576	=COUNTA(INDIRECT("Sheet13!1:1048576"))				
13	=Sheet14!1:1048576	=COUNTA(INDIRECT("Sheet14!1:1048576"))				
14	=Sheet15!1:1048576	=COUNTA(INDIRECT("Sheet15!1:1048576"))				
15	=Sheet16!1:1048576	=COUNTA(INDIRECT("Sheet16!1:1048576"))				

The formula in B1 is

="=COUNTA(INDIRECT("""&MID(A1,2,255)&"""))"

This is understood by Excel to simply be a bunch of text made to *look* like a formula, but it does not *act* like one. Since it looks like the right one, let's copy/paste special values (by the trick of right-dragging the border away & back to the same spot which gives a dropdown to choose values):

=COUNTA(INDIRECT("Sheet2!1:1048576"))	
=COUNTA(INDIRECT("Sheet3!1:1048576"))	
=COUNTA(INDIRECT("Sheet4!1:1048576"))	
=COUNTA(INDIRECT("Sheet5!1:1048576"))	
=COUNTA(INDIRECT("Sheet6!1:1048576"))	
=COUNTA(INDIRECT("Sheet7!1:1048576"))	
=COUNTA(INDIRECT("Sheet8!1:1048576"))	
=COUNTA(INDIRECT("Sheet9!1:1048576"))	Move Here
=COUNTA(INDIRECT("Sheet10!1:1048576'	Copy Here
=COUNTA(INDIRECT("Sheet11!1:1048576'	Copy Here as Values Only
=COUNTA(INDIRECT("Sheet12!1:1048576'	Copy Here as Formats Only
=COUNTA(INDIRECT("Sheet13!1:1048576'	Link Here
=COUNTA(INDIRECT("Sheet14!1:1048576'	Create Hyperlink Here
=COUNTA(INDIRECT("Sheet15!1:1048576'	Shift Down and Copy
=COUNTA(INDIRECT("Sheet16!1:1048576'	Shift Right and Copy

So now it *looks* like the formula we want, even in the formula bar:

▾	⋮	×	✓	*fx*	'=COUNTA(INDIRECT("Sheet2!1:1048576"))

B	C	D
=COUNTA(INDIRECT("Sheet2!1:1048576"))		
=COUNTA(INDIRECT("Sheet3!1:1048576"))		
=COUNTA(INDIRECT("Sheet4!1:1048576"))		
=COUNTA(INDIRECT("Sheet5!1:1048576"))		
=COUNTA(INDIRECT("Sheet6!1:1048576"))		
=COUNTA(INDIRECT("Sheet7!1:1048576"))		
=COUNTA(INDIRECT("Sheet8!1:1048576"))		

But it's not. We once again need to remove the leading quote (text-to-columns is easiest):

| | | | fx | =COUNTA(INDIRECT("Sheet2!1:1048576")) | | |

B	C	D	E	F	G
1					
0					
1					
1					
1					
1					
1					
1					
1					
1					
1					
1					
1					
1					
1					

Changing cell reference

If you have a reference such as =SUM(A500:A525) and need to change it to
=SUM(A525:A535), you would most likely edit the formula and change the 500
to 525 and the 525 to 535. And of course, that would work. Did you know you
can just change the 500 to 535 and get the same result? That is, you would see
this before pressing enter:

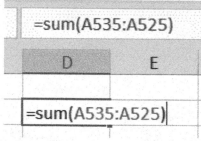

but as soon as you entered the formula, you'd see:

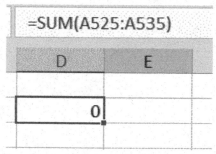

Excel would change it for you!

Numbering entries tip

Look at the following:

A4		▼	:	× ✓ f_x	=MAX($A$1:A3)+1	
	A	B	C	D	E	F
1	Number Tip					
2		1	Here's some text			
3						
4		2	Here's some more text			
5						
6		3	Perhaps this could be a question which takes			
7			more than one line to pose			
8						
9		4	And another question			
10						
11		5	And yet another			
12						

You can see that the formula looks at all numbers from A1 (as an absolute reference) to the cell above (as a relative reference), and adds one to the largest number on that range. In this case, cell A4 has a formula which examines A1:A3 and takes the largest # (1) and adds 1 to it. So far, no big deal. This formula is *not* being filled down, but is copy/pasted to the first line of each "paragraph". The nice feature with this formula, instead of simply entering the numbers wanted, is that if you decide to delete a question or add a new one, all the other numbers are re-numbered! Let's see what happens when rows 6:8 are deleted:

Number Tip						Σ AutoSum
	1	Here's some text			Delete Format	⬇ Fill ▾ ◇ Clear ▾
	2	Here's some more text			▦ Delete Cells...	
	3	Perhaps this could be a question which takes			⇛ Delete Sheet Rows	
		more than one line to pose			⬚ Delete Sheet Columns	
					▦ Delete Sheet	
	4	And another question				
	5	And yet another				

The result is:

| A6 | | | ▾ | ⋮ | × | ✓ | *fx* | =MAX($A$1:A5)+1 |

	A	B	C	D	E	F
1	Number Tip					
2	1	Here's some text				
3						
4	2	Here's some more text				
5						
6	3	And another question				
7						
8	4	And yet another				

Notice that cell A6 has the same formula as it did before, but what *were* questions 4 and 5 are now 3 and 4! Suppose I wanted to insert a new question before question 4 (let's also assume there are 100 questions!)

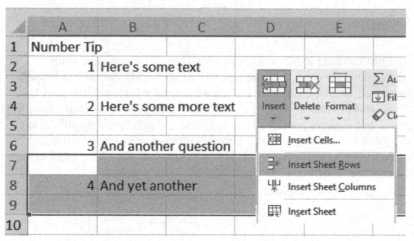

Now we have:

	A	B	C	D
1	Number Tip			
2	1	Here's some text		
3				
4	2	Here's some more text		
5				
6	3	And another question		
7				
8				
9				
10				
11	4	And yet another		
12				

I type in the new statement and copy/paste any of the formulas in column A to cell A8:

A8			▼ ⋮ ✕ ✓ f_x		=MAX($A$1:A7)+1	
	A	B	C	D	E	F
1	Number Tip					
2	1	Here's some text				
3						
4	2	Here's some more text				
5						
6	3	And another question				
7						
8	4	the new statement				
9						
10						
11	5	And yet another				
12						

FORMATTING

Removing the leading apostrophe from many cells at once.

You may have noticed that you can't find/replace ' with nothing if it's the leading apostrophe that you want to clear because Excel "thinks" it's not there in the first place!

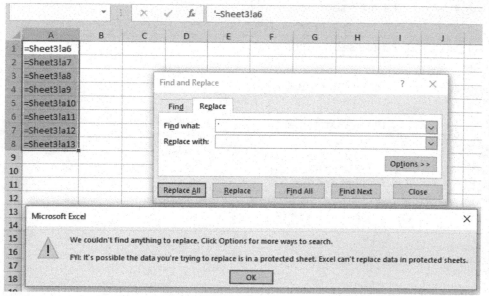

You can see in the formula bar that this *does* begin with an apostrophe, but it doesn't show in cell A1. In fact, A1:A8 all begin with a leading quote/apostrophe in this example.

You can remove them all by copying an unformatted, empty cell and using Paste Special, and selecting the "Add" option:

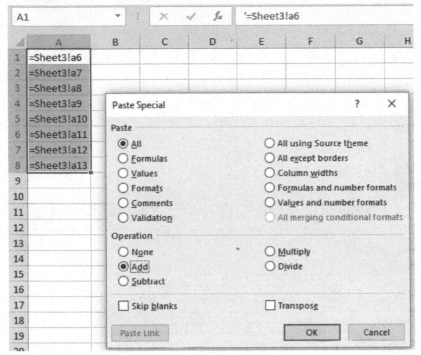

And you see the result:

But something's wrong here. These should all return a value, not the formula! Well, they're still text and need to be re-entered. This can be done by using something in common in all the cells (often will be an "=", but could be a letter, like "s" in this example) and replacing that character with itself:

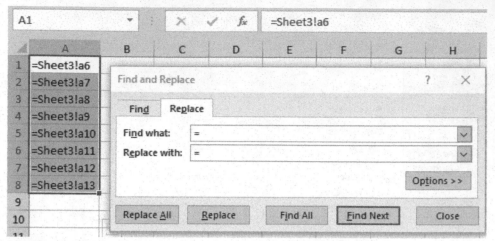

The result:

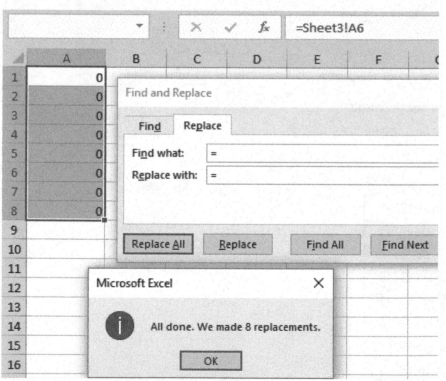

You can see A1:A8 are now all calculated.

You can also do *all* the above in one easy step! Select A1:A8, use Data/ Text-to-Columns, and simple click Finish!!

Window/Arrange Tiled (except this one!)

Here's the result of using Window/Arrange/Tiled with 3 open workbooks:

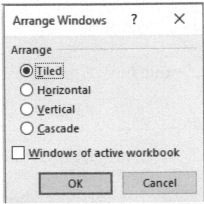

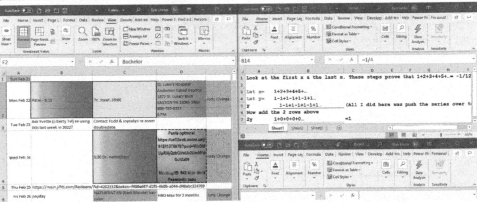

But suppose you didn't want to include Infinity.xlsx (top/right window) in the arrangement? Do you have to close it or hide it? No, you can minimize it (click the leftmost tool in the upper-right corner of the workbook:

and it won't be included in the arrangement:

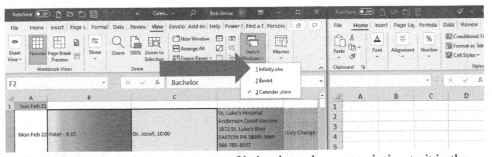

Notice Infinity.xlsx (shown as an open file by the red arrow pointing to it in the Switch Windows ribbon command) is not included in the arrangement, yet it's still open!

MISCELLANEOUS

Returning from clicking on a hyperlink
Once you click a hyperlink, you can return to the source by pressing Alt/Left arrow!

You can type R1C1 notation into the Name box:

R3C1000

	L	M	N
1			
2			
3			

and when I hit enter:

	ALL	AL

I guess column ALL is column 1000!

Play a trick on your coworkers by hiding even row numbers
What happened to the even row numbers?

A1	▼

	A	B	C
1			
3			
5			
7			

How to do this is select a cell in row 2 and give it a font of 120-pt size. Say that was B2. Select B1:B2 and use the fill handle to drag down 50 rows or so.

It'll look like this:

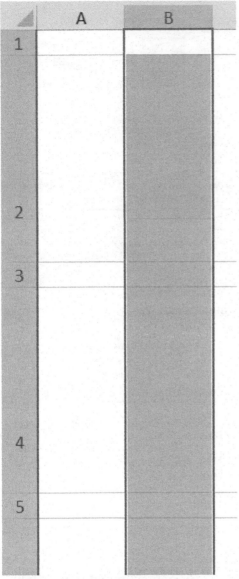

Now select everything (click on the triangle above row 1 and to the left of column A), and change the row height to 20 or so. That's all there is to it!

Another one: Go to your coworker's computer, select all cells and format them as ;;;

Now, whatever is typed will disappear!

Print Area manipulation

To clear the Print Area you can either *set* the Print Area when all cells are selected, or choose the Clear Print Area command.

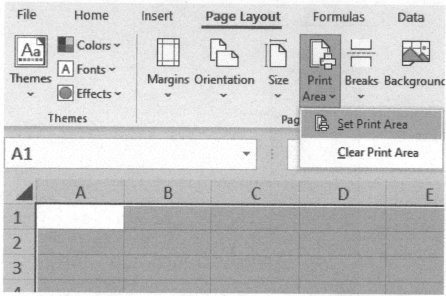

Did you know that if you already have a print area and want to *add* another range to it, another choice shows up?:

	A	B	C	D	E	F
1	Print me too	Print me too	Print me too			
2	Print me too	Print me too	Print me too			
3	Print me too	Print me too	Print me too			
4	Print me too	Print me too	Print me too			
5	Print me too	Print me too	Print me too			
6						
7						
8						
9			Print me	Print me	Print me	Print me
10			Print me	Print me	Print me	Print me
11			Print me	Print me	Print me	Print me
12			Print me	Print me	Print me	Print me
13			Print me	Print me	Print me	Print me
14			Print me	Print me	Print me	Print me

Here. C9:F14 is the print area. If you select A1:C5, you can see a new command:

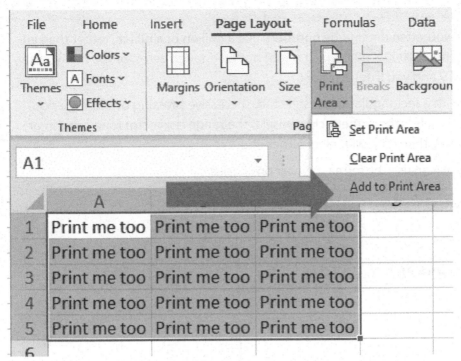

Change Rows to Repeat at Top On All Worksheets

Even if you open the Page Setup dialog while in group mode, you can not change the Rows to Repeat at Top on multiple worksheets at one time.

This macro will set the rows to repeat to rows 1 & 2 for all sheets in the active workbook:

```
Sub ChangeRowsToRepeatAtTop()
    Dim WS As Worksheet
    For Each WS In ActiveWorkbook.Worksheets
        WS.PageSetup.PrintTitleRows = "$1:$2"
    Next WS
End Sub
```

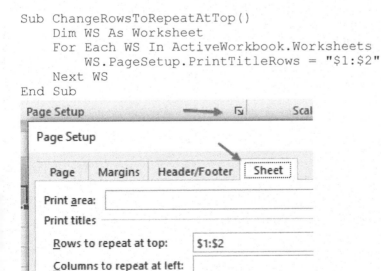

To change Columns to Repeat at Left, use .PrintTitleColumns = "$A:$B".

A few miscellaneous tips & tricks

- If you often enter large numbers, like a million or a billion, rather than entering 1000000000, which might not be enough zeros, or too many, enter 1E9 and you'll get 1 billion!

- With a rectangular range selected, successive pressing of \Ctrl/. (period) will select the corners, clockwise! If the range is a vector (one column or row), then ctrl/. will select either end.

- You can use the format painter on shapes.

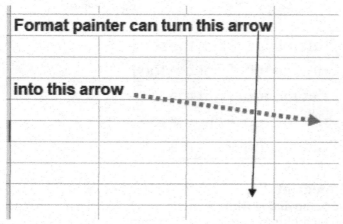

Click the red one, click the format painter, click the black one!

How can you merge A1:E1, A2:E2, etc., down to A100:E100 easily?

	A	B	C	D	E
1	How did I merge each row A:E?				
2					
3					
4					
5					
6					
7					
8					

Select A1:E100, and issue this command:

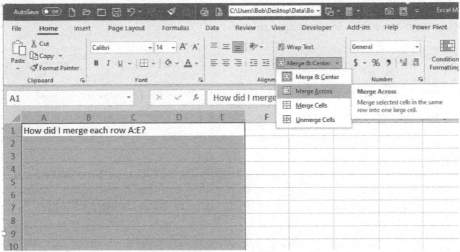

Near the Merge & Center command in the ribbon is a little dropdown arrow. Click on this and select "Merge Across" and it does just what you want in this example!

More miscellaneous tips:

- Ctrl/' (single quote) – this copies the cell above exactly. So, if cell A1 has =SUM($B2:C7), then pressing Ctrl/' from cell A2 will put =SUM($B2:C7) in cell A2.

- Ctrl/" (double-quote) – this copies the value from the cell above. So, if cell A1 has =SUM(E1:E10) and it's value is 350, then pressing Ctrl/" from cell A2 will put the plain number 350 in cell A2.

- Ctrl/; will put in today's date

- Ctrl/: will put in the time.

- If you press Ctrl/; followed by a space then Ctrl/:, you'll have the date and the time.

- Shift/F2 will insert a Note (previously known as Comment before Threaded Comments were introduced.

Fill Handle technique to skip percentage columns

Suppose you have data laid out like this:

	A	B	C	D	E	F	G	H	I	J	K	L	M	N	O	
1		Jan	% of Q Total	Feb	% of Q Total	Mar	% of Q Total	Q1	Apr	% of Q Total	May	% of Q Total	Jun	% of Q Total	Q2	Jul
2		285	17.4%	857	52.4%	492	30.1%	1634	582	35.8%	272	16.7%	771	47.4%	1625	6
3		353	65.5%	49	9.1%	137	25.4%	539	704	33.0%	912	42.8%	516	24.2%	2132	1
4		232	16.5%	986	70.0%	191	13.6%	1409	461	33.6%	326	23.8%	585	42.6%	1372	2
5		623	60.5%	173	16.8%	234	22.7%	1030	286	27.6%	402	38.8%	347	33.5%	1035	6
6		932	48.5%	280	14.6%	711	37.0%	1923	369	20.1%	869	47.3%	598	32.6%	1836	
7		933	43.2%	512	23.7%	716	33.1%	2161	16	2.3%	564	79.4%	130	18.3%	710	8
8		350	18.8%	826	44.4%	685	36.8%	1861	156	13.4%	874	75.0%	136	11.7%	1166	8
9	Total	3708														
10																

That is, the pattern is Month, %, Month, %, Month, %, Qtr total then that repeats. This goes out to column AC. You want to put the total, like in B9, to all the appropriate columns. You can't use the fill handle from B9 because you'd get:

	A	B	C	D	E	F	G	H	I	J
1		Jan	% of Q Total	Feb	% of Q Total	Mar	% of Q Total	Q1	Apr	% of Q Total
2		285	17.4%	857	52.4%	492	30.1%	1634	582	35.8%
3		353	65.5%	49	9.1%	137	25.4%	539	704	33.0%
4		232	16.5%	986	70.0%	191	13.6%	1409	461	33.6%
5		623	60.5%	173	16.8%	234	22.7%	1030	286	27.6%
6		932	48.5%	280	14.6%	711	37.0%	1923	369	20.1%
7		933	43.2%	512	23.7%	716	33.1%	2161	16	2.3%
8		350	18.8%	826	44.4%	685	36.8%	1861	156	13.4%
9	Total	3708	2.7033201	3683	2.3095177	3166	1.9871621	10557	2574	1.6580009

...etc., and you don't want the total of the percent columns. So, you select B9:C9 (while C9 is blank) and use the fill handle:

	A	B	C	D	E	F	G	H	I	J
1		Jan	% of Q Total	Feb	% of Q Total	Mar	% of Q Total	Q1	Apr	% of Q Total
2		285	17.4%	857	52.4%	492	30.1%	1634	582	35.8%
3		353	65.5%	49	9.1%	137	25.4%	539	704	33.0%
4		232	16.5%	986	70.0%	191	13.6%	1409	461	33.6%
5		623	60.5%	173	16.8%	234	22.7%	1030	286	27.6%
6		932	48.5%	280	14.6%	711	37.0%	1923	369	20.1%
7		933	43.2%	512	23.7%	716	33.1%	2161	16	2.3%
8		350	18.8%	826	44.4%	685	36.8%	1861	156	13.4%
9	Total	3708		3683		3166		10557		1.6580009

..etc., and it starts off okay. But because of the Q1 total, the pattern is broken and again you get a total in column J and don't want one there.

The solution is to select B9:C9 and use the fill handle through H9:

▲	A	B	C	D	E	F	G	H	I	J
1		Jan	% of Q Total	Feb	% of Q Total	Mar	% of Q Total	Q1	Apr	% of Q
2		285	17.4%	857	52.4%	492	30.1%	1634	582	3
3		353	65.5%	49	9.1%	137	25.4%	539	704	3
4		232	16.5%	986	70.0%	191	13.6%	1409	461	3
5		623	60.5%	173	16.8%	234	22.7%	1030	286	2
6		932	48.5%	280	14.6%	711	37.0%	1923	369	2
7		933	43.2%	512	23.7%	716	33.1%	2161	16	
8		350	18.8%	826	44.4%	685	36.8%	1861	156	1
9	Total	3708		3683		3166		10557		

Then, with *that* selection (B9:H9), drag the fill handle to AC9:

▲	K	L	M	N	O	P	Q	R	S	T	U	V	W	X	Y	Z	AA	AB	AC
1	May	% of Q Total	Jun	% of Q Total	Q2	Jul	% of Q Total	Aug	% of Q Total	Sep	% of Q Total	Q3	Oct	% of Q Total	Nov	% of Q Total	Dec	% of Q Total	Q4
2	272	16.7%	771	47.4%	1625	633	53.1%	511	42.9%	48	4.0%	1192	616	28.4%	921	42.5%	632	29.1%	2169
3	912	42.8%	516	24.2%	2132	171	16.4%	431	41.4%	438	42.1%	1040	251	26.5%	310	32.8%	385	40.7%	946
4	326	23.8%	585	42.6%	1372	263	14.1%	953	50.9%	655	35.0%	1871	561	26.7%	957	45.6%	581	27.7%	2099
5	402	38.8%	347	33.5%	1035	690	45.5%	476	31.4%	350	23.1%	1516	967	42.3%	531	23.2%	786	34.4%	2284
6	869	47.3%	598	32.6%	1836	8	0.9%	525	60.7%	332	38.4%	865	456	28.1%	469	28.9%	699	43.0%	1624
7	564	79.4%	130	18.3%	710	893	69.3%	268	20.8%	127	9.9%	1288	202	15.2%	684	51.3%	447	33.5%	1333
8	874	75.0%	136	11.7%	1166	890	72.5%	260	21.2%	78	6.4%	1228	584	29.8%	596	30.4%	779	39.8%	1959
9	4219		3083		9876	3548		3424		2028		9000	3637		4468		4309		12414

Distributing

Suppose you need to fill the cells between row 1 and 15 evenly:

	C
1	123
2	
3	
4	
5	
6	
7	
8	
9	
10	
11	
12	
13	
14	
15	554

You can do it by adding 30.78571 to each cell:

=(C15-C1)/(ROW(C15)-ROW(C1))

E	F	G
30.78571		

But instead of having to figure this out, Excel "knows" it automatically! Simply select C1:C15, then use Home/Editing/Fill/Series:

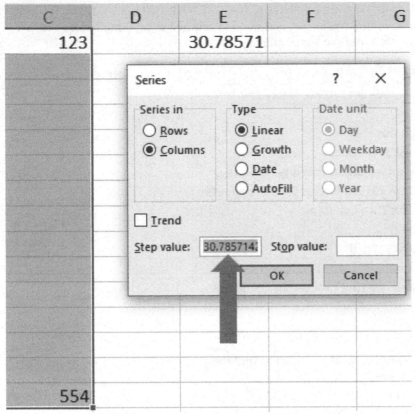

And Excel already has this filled for you! You just need to click OK!

4 Ways to remove everything before the colon "puzzle"

Suppose you have this worksheet and need to remove everything before the ":",
including the colon *and* the space after it.

	A	B
1	Task -- remove everything before the ":"	
2		
3	Test1: Do this	
4	Here's test 2: Do that.	
5	For your information: This is good stuff	
6	Here's Item #3: Don't forget the doughnuts!	
7	And finally: The Final Item	
8	Test1: Do this	
9	Here's test 2: Do that.	
10	For your information: This is good stuff	
11	Here's Item #3: Don't forget the doughnuts!	
12	And finally: The Final Item	

Method 1, using a formula:

Okay, what formula? Well, we need to find the position of the colon, so the formula in B3 does that:

B3		× ✓ *fx*	=FIND(":",A3)

	A	B
3	Test1: Do this	6
4	Here's test 2: Do that.	
5	For your information: This is good stuff	
6	Here's Item #3: Don't forget the doughnuts!	

The position of the colon in A3 is 6. Given that, we can add 2 to it to get to the
first character we want to keep (this *does* assume each colon is followed by a
space). Then we can use the MID function to get the rest:

B3		× ✓ *fx*	=MID(A3,FIND(":",A3)+2,255)

	A	B	C
3	Test1: Do this	Do this	
4	Here's test 2: Do that.	Do that.	
5	For your information: This is good stuff	This is good stuff	
6	Here's Item #3: Don't forget the doughnuts!	Don't forget the doughnuts!	
7	And finally: The Final Item	The Final Item	

Of course, this is filled down, and we're done (unless the result is to be in column
A, in which we can copy column B and paste special values to column A, and
finally clear column B!)

Method 2, using Text-to-Columns:

Select the data in column A, and bring up Data/Text-to-Columns:

Making sure Delimited is selected in step 1, clicking Next brings us to step 2:

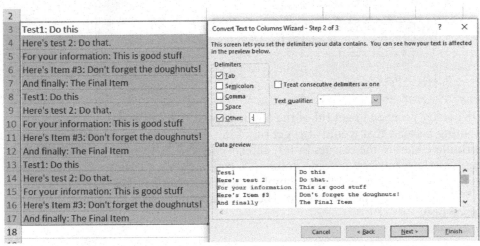

Enter a colon in the "Other" checkbox, and you can see the preview looks good (aside from a leading space).

Click Next, and in step 3, select Do not import column (skip):

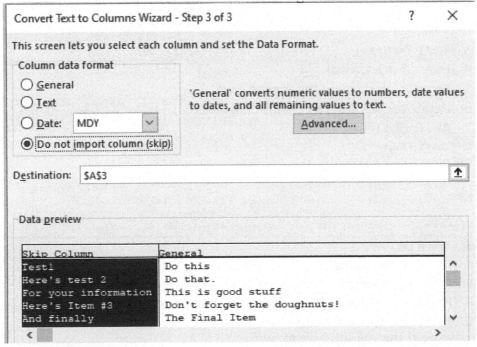

Now click Finish:

3	Do this
4	Do that.
5	This is good stuff
6	Don't forget the doughnuts!
7	The Final Item
8	Do this
9	Do that

OK, lastly we need to get rid of the leading space. We can't replace space with nothing because that would also get rid of the spaces between words. So another formula comes to the rescue. In B3, enter =MID(A3,2,255) and fill down. Then copy, paste special values onto column A, and lastly clear column B! An alternate to the MID function, just to be complete here, is to use =SUBSTITUTE(A3," "," ",1) in B3 and repeat as before. The 1 in the formula says to replace the *first* space only.

Method 3, using Flash Fill:

Enter what you want to see in cell B3, without a formula:

B3	▼ : × ✓ ƒx	Do this

	A	B
3	Test1: Do this	Do this
4	Here's test 2: Do that.	
5	For your information: This is good stuff	
6	Here's Item #3: Don't forget the doughnuts!	
7	And finally: The Final Item	
8	Test1: Do this	

Now press Ctrl/E (flash fill):

B3	▼ : × ✓ ƒx	Do this

	A	B
3	Test1: Do this	Do this
4	Here's test 2: Do that.	Do that.
5	For your information: This is good stuff	This is good stuff
6	Here's Item #3: Don't forget the doughnuts!	Don't forget the doughnuts!
7	And finally: The Final Item	The Final Item

Pretty sweet! But you still have to cut/paste B to A.

Method 4 (my favorite), using Replace:

Select the data in column A, and use Ctrl/H (replace). In the Find what, enter "*:
" (without the quotes) – the * is the wildcard and says find everything until and
including a colon and a space. Replace this with nothing, clicking Replace All:

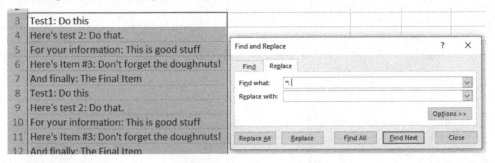

The result:

3	Do this
4	Do that.
5	This is good stuff
6	Don't forget the doughnuts!
7	The Final Item
8	Do this

It's my favorite because there's no involving column B. After the replace, we're
finished!

What's so special about viewing your spreadsheet at 39% or less?

Using View/Zoom, and picking 40%,

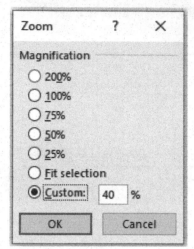

this spreadsheet shows nothing special aside from the range called "This" is selected:

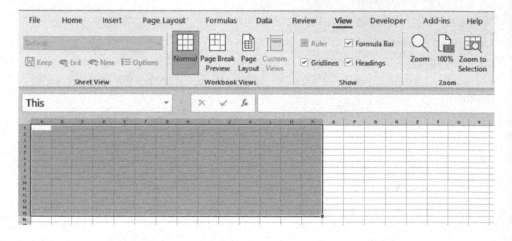

There are two other ranges, called "is", and "Cool". At 39% or less, some magic appears:

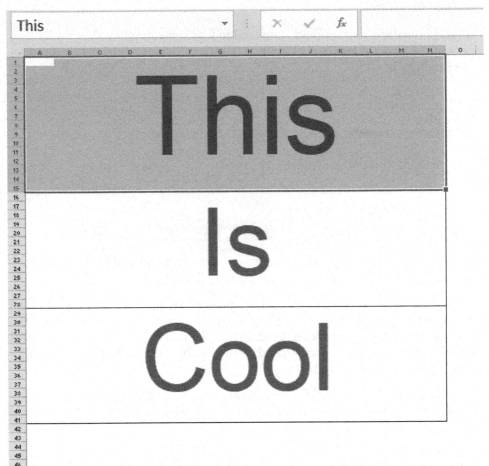

Range names on the active sheet show up! Range names which are one cell only will not show up, and neither will dynamic ranges, like something based on OFFSET. But when you inherit someone's file, this is a good technique to get a quick look at the range names used and their references!

Finding after the Find dialog is closed
Shift/F4 repeats the last find after a find command was done; Shift/Ctrl/F4 repeats find backwards!

That is, if you did a normal Find command to find something:

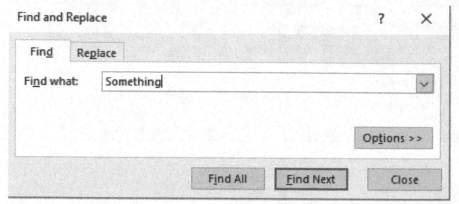

then if you close the find command and use Shift/F4, it will still find the same text, and Shift/Ctrl/F4 will find the same text backwards.

Note that F4 repeats the last command. If you do close the dialog, you could Find Next by pressing F4. But, if you are doing some formatting of some found cells (for instance, changing the font to bold...), then F4 will repeat the Bold command instead of repeating the Find command. However, Shift/F4 and Ctrl/Shift/F4 will repeat the last Find command.

If you need to press Shift/Ctrl/F4 several times and find the keystroke unwieldy, press it once and then use F4 several times to repeat the Shift/Ctrl/F4 command.

Understanding the order of View/Arrange All

Suppose you have 5 workbooks open and you use View/Arrange All/Tiled:

The top/left window will always be the active window. But what is the order of the rest of them? Probably seemed sort of random, didn't it? Well, here's the "secret" of how to determine the sequence. If I wanted to see it in this order:

Book1	Book4	Book3
	Book5	Book2

...all I need do is click the workbooks in the reverse order, from bottom right (book2) and up (book3, then book5, then book4, then book1). Yes, just click! The result:

So, it turns out, that Excel's order always was the LIFO (Last in, first out) sequence you activated the windows. Go figure!

Using the buried feature: Home/Editing/Fill/Justify

What is this command, anyway? It's a way of re-flowing text. Suppose you have text like this...

	A	B	C	D	E	F	G	H	I	J	K	L	M	N
1	Now is the time for all good men to come to the aid of their party. Now is the time for all good men to come to the aid of their party.													
2														
3														

...and you want to fit it all from columns A:E, not A:N. Make the selection as this:

	A	B	C	D	E	F	G	H	I	J	K	L	M	N
1	Now is the time for all good men to come to the aid of their party. Now is the time for all good men to come to the aid of their party.													
2														
3														
4														
5														

purposely selecting a few extra rows, then issuing the command Home/Editing/Fill/Justify:

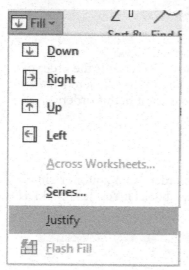

...and the result is:

	A	B	C	D	E
1	Now is the	time for all good men to come to the			
2	aid of their	party. Now is the time for all good men			
3	to come to	the aid of their party.			

...just what you wanted. If you selected A1:C2 first, you would see an Excel warning message:

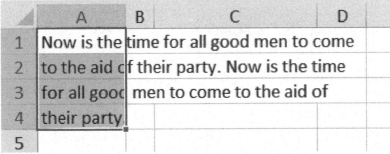

...which means all the text won't fit inside A1:C2. If that's ok with you, then you'd see:

	A	B	C
1	Now is the	time for all good men to	
2	come to th	e aid of their party. Now	
3	is the time	for all good men to come	
4	to the aid c	f their party.	
5			

You can also use Home/Editing/Fill/Justify to flow the text into a longer string, rather than shorter strings. If you select A1:D4 from the above and use Home/Editing/Fill/Justify, then you'd see the text reflowed to:

	A	B	C	D
1	Now is the	time for all good men to come		
2	to the aid c	f their party. Now is the time		
3	for all good	men to come to the aid of		
4	their party.			
5				

And if you selected A1:K4, it would reflow back to the original:

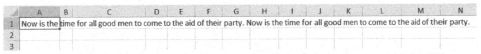

Just to be complete, if instead of A1:K4 being just selected you tried A1:K3, (leaving out row 4):

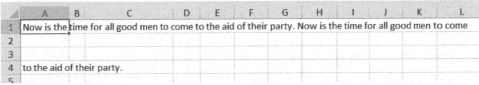

Then this is probably not what you want!

Shift/Scrolling

You probably know that scrolling is "localized". If your entire worksheet goes from A1:C10, the scrollbar looks like this:

But if your last cell were X20000, it'd look like this:

Notice the difference in the sizes of both the vertical and horizontal scrollbars between the two diagrams. It gives you a hint as to the size of the worksheet. A cute tip in itself, if you didn't know it.

If you simply scroll by dragging either scrollbar, you're somewhat restricted to the range where there is data. This makes sense. However, if you *do* want to scroll faster, and outside the range of the data, simply hold the shift key down as you scroll. You'll get to row 1048576 or column XFD pretty quickly!

Drag/Scrolling

Did you know that if, in a large worksheet, you drag the cursor – that is, you click in cell A20, for example, hold the mouse button down and then drag the cursor beyond the bottom of the worksheet, into the area of the tabs or over the scroll-bars, the worksheet scrolls. But did you know that the farther away the cursor is from the window the faster it scrolls?

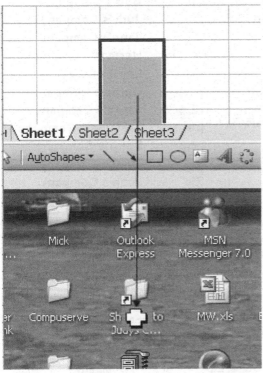

If you resize the Excel application window (here you see part of my desktop) and drag totally outside the window, Excel's worksheet will scroll very fast.

Mailing Label tricks - 1

Suppose you have a list of names & addresses arranged like this and you want to rearrange it like the textbox indicates:

	A	B	C
1	Address	City...	Company
2	Bob's Address	Bob's City, State, Zip	Bob's Company
3	Judy's Address	Judy's City, State, Zip	Judy's Company
4	Jane's Address	Jane's City, State, Zip	Jane's Company
5	Herman's Address	Herman's City, State, Zip	Herman's Company
6	Laird's Address	Zip	Laird's Company
7	Curtis's Address	, Zip	Curtis's Company
8	Jared's Address	Zip	Jared's Company
9	Stefanie's Address	te, Zip	Stefanie's Company
10	Peter's Address	Zip	Peter's Company
11	Alice's Address	Zip	Alice's Company
12	Joan's Address	Zip	Joan's Company
13	Reid's Address	Zip	Reid's Company
14	LaVerne's Address	te, Zip	LaVerne's Company
15	Eli's Address	Eli's City, State, Zip	Eli's Company
16	Don's Address	Don's City, State, Zip	Don's Company

From this, we want:
Bob's Company
Bob's Address
Bob's City, State Zip

Judy's Company
Judy's Address
Judy's City, State Zip

etc

If you tried to enter formulas like these in D2:D4 (showing formulas):

	A	B	C	D
1	Address	City...	Company	
2	Bob's Address	Bob's City, State, Zip	Bob's Company	=C2
3	Judy's Address	Judy's City, State, Zip	Judy's Company	=A2
4	Jane's Address	Jane's City, State, Zip	Jane's Company	=B2
5	Herman's Address	Herman's City, State, Zip	Herman's Company	
6	Laird's Address	Laird's City, State, Zip	Laird's Company	

which results in:

	A	B	C	D
1	Address	City...	Company	
2	Bob's Address	Bob's City, State, Zip	Bob's Company	Bob's Company
3	Judy's Address	Judy's City, State, Zip	Judy's Company	Bob's Address
4	Jane's Address	Jane's City, State, Zip	Jane's Company	Bob's City, State, Zip
5	Herman's Address	Herman's City, State, Zip	Herman's Company	
6	Laird's Address	Laird's City, State, Zip	Laird's Company	
7	Curtis's Address	Curtis's City, State, Zip	Curtis's Company	

which seems like a good start, filling this down (starting with selecting D2:D5, including a blank cell) produces a disaster:

`=C6`

	B	C	D
	City...	Company	
	Bob's City, State, Zip	Bob's Company	Bob's Company
	Judy's City, State, Zip	Judy's Company	Bob's Address
	Jane's City, State, Zip	Jane's Company	Bob's City, State, Zip
	Herman's City, State, Zip	Herman's Company	
	Laird's City, State, Zip	Laird's Company	Laird's Company
	Curtis's City, State, Zip	Curtis's Company	Laird's Address
	Jared's City, State, Zip	Jared's Company	Laird's City, State, Zip
	Stefanie's City, State, Zip	Stefanie's Company	
	Peter's City, State, Zip	Peter's Company	Peter's Company
	Alice's City, State, Zip	Alice's Company	Peter's Address
	Joan's City, State, Zip	Joan's Company	Peter's City, State, Zip
	Reid's City, State, Zip	Reid's Company	

---what happened to the intermediate companies like in row 3, 4, and 5? (Judy's company...) – notice the formula bar for the active cell has =C6 in it, not =C3. Here are the formulas for the next few rows:

D6 ▾ f_x =C6

	C	D
1	Company	
2	Bob's Company	=C2
3	Judy's Company	=A2
4	Jane's Company	=B2
5	Herman's Company	
6	Laird's Company	=C6
7	Curtis's Company	=A6
8	Jared's Company	=B6
9	Stefanie's Company	
10	Peter's Company	=C10
11	Alice's Company	=A10
12	Joan's Company	=B10
13	Reid's Company	
14	LaVerne's Company	=C14
15	Eli's Company	=A14
16	Don's Company	=B14

You begin to get the picture.

The solution? Watch: Enter these values (not formulas!):

	A	B	C	D
	D2	▼	*fx*	xc2
1	Address	City...	Company	
2	Bob's Address	Bob's City, State, Zip	Bob's Company	xc2
3	Judy's Address	Judy's City, State, Zip	Judy's Company	xa2
4	Jane's Address	Jane's City, State, Zip	Jane's Company	xb2
5	Herman's Address	Herman's City, State, Zip	Herman's Company	
6	Laird's Address	Laird's City, State, Zip	Laird's Company	

Now, when you select D2:D5 (yes, D6 is blank) and double-click the fill handle, you get this:

	A	B	C	D
	D2	▼	*fx*	xc2
1	Address	City...	Company	
2	Bob's Address	Bob's City, State, Zip	Bob's Company	xc2
3	Judy's Address	Judy's City, State, Zip	Judy's Company	xa2
4	Jane's Address	Jane's City, State, Zip	Jane's Company	xb2
5	Herman's Address	Herman's City, State, Zip	Herman's Company	
6	Laird's Address	Laird's City, State, Zip	Laird's Company	xc3
7	Curtis's Address	Curtis's City, State, Zip	Curtis's Company	xa3
8	Jared's Address	Jared's City, State, Zip	Jared's Company	xb3
9	Stefanie's Address	Stefanie's City, State, Zip	Stefanie's Company	
10	Peter's Address	Peter's City, State, Zip	Peter's Company	xc4
11	Alice's Address	Alice's City, State, Zip	Alice's Company	xa4
12	Joan's Address	Joan's City, State, Zip	Joan's Company	xb4

Now you can change x to =:

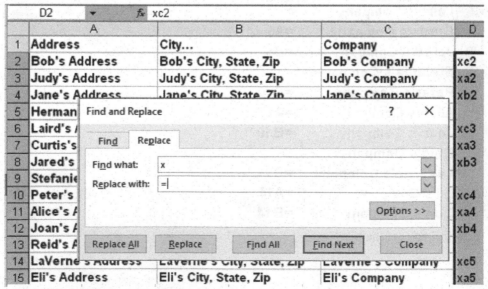

	A	B	C	D
	D2	▼	*fx*	xc2
1	Address	City...	Company	
2	Bob's Address	Bob's City, State, Zip	Bob's Company	xc2
3	Judy's Address	Judy's City, State, Zip	Judy's Company	xa2
4	Jane's Address	Jane's City, State, Zip	Jane's Company	xb2
5	Herman			
6	Laird's A			xc3
7	Curtis's			xa3
8	Jared's			xb3
9	Stefanie			
10	Peter's			xc4
11	Alice's A			xa4
12	Joan's A			xb4
13	Reid's A			
14	LaVerne's Address	LaVerne's City, State, Zip	LaVerne's Company	xc5
15	Eli's Address	Eli's City, State, Zip	Eli's Company	xa5

Find and Replace   ?   ✕

Find   Replace

Find what: x

Replace with: =|

Options >>

Replace All   Replace   Find All   Find Next   Close

This gives (formulas are showing)

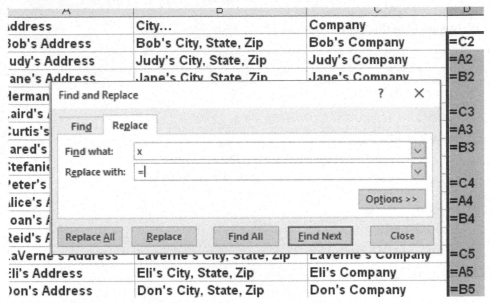

	A	B	C	D
	ddress	City...	Company	
	3ob's Address	Bob's City, State, Zip	Bob's Company	=C2
	udy's Address	Judy's City, State, Zip	Judy's Company	=A2
	ane's Address	Jane's City, State, Zip	Jane's Company	=B2
	lerman			=C3
	aird's			=A3
	:urtis's			=B3
	ared's			=C4
	itefanie			
	'eter's			=A4
	lice's			=B4
	oan's			
	{eid's			=C5
	aVerne's Address	LaVerne's City, State, Zip	LaVerne's Company	=A5
	:li's Address	Eli's City, State, Zip	Eli's Company	=B5
	)on's Address	Don's City, State, Zip	Don's Company	

Find and Replace ? X

Find | Replace

Find what: x

Replace with: =|

Options >>

Replace All | Replace | Find All | Find Next | Close

And without formulas showing, we have:

D6   ▼   *fx*   =C3

	A	B	C	D
1	Address	City...	Company	
2	Bob's Address	Bob's City, State, Zip	Bob's Company	Bob's Company
3	Judy's Address	Judy's City, State, Zip	Judy's Company	Bob's Address
4	Jane's Address	Jane's City, State, Zip	Jane's Company	Bob's City, State, Zip
5	Herman's Address	Herman's City, State, Zip	Herman's Company	
6	Laird's Address	Laird's City, State, Zip	Laird's Company	Judy's Company
7	Curtis's Address	Curtis's City, State, Zip	Curtis's Company	Judy's Address
8	Jared's Address	Jared's City, State, Zip	Jared's Company	Judy's City, State, Zip
9	Stefanie's Address	Stefanie's City, State, Zip	Stefanie's Company	
10	Peter's Address	Peter's City, State, Zip	Peter's Company	Jane's Company
11	Alice's Address	Alice's City, State, Zip	Alice's Company	Jane's Address
12	Joan's Address	Joan's City, State, Zip	Joan's Company	Jane's City, State, Zip
13	Reid's Address	Reid's City, State, Zip	Reid's Company	

Sneaky, eh?

But this was touted as mailing labels. The *format* is okay, but how can you make these fit on address label paper? Well, you can tweak the row height of the blank cells. First, you need to make column D be the print area, from the top label to the last line of the bottom label. Check how it would look now, using Print Preview. Make sure there are no labels which are split across pages. You can also adjust the top & bottom margins. If it needs adjustment, select column D, use Home/Find & Select/Go To Special, select Blanks, and click OK. Now only the blanks are selected. Now use Home/Format/Row Height and make your adjustment, taller or smaller and print preview again.

Mailing Label tricks - 2

OK, what about this set of addresses?

	A	B	C	D
1	Jones, Jim			
2	addr1			
3	city1, State1 Zip1			
4				
5	Smith, Bill			
6	Addr2			
7	Addr2 part2			
8	City2, State2 Zip2			
9	emailaddr			
10				
11	Johnson, Alice			
12	addr3			
13	Cityt3, State3 Zip3			
14	email1			
15	email2			
16	POBox 3333			
17				
18	Zedwick, Paul			
19	addr4			
20	City4, State4 Zip4			
21				
22	Bergman, Sylvia			
23	addr5			
24	City5, State5 Zip5			

How can you possibly sort these by last name?

It's already "arranged", but what if you need to sort them by last name? Not only does this seem impossible, but the number of lines in each address is not the same, making it more difficult! Or so it would seem!

First, we need to insert a row at the top:

◢	A	B
1		
2	Jones, Jim	
3	addr1	
4	city1, State1 Zip1	
5		How can y
6	Smith, Bill	these by la
7	Addr2	
8	Addr2 part2	
9	City2, State2 Zip2	
10	emailaddr	
11		
12	Johnson, Alice	
13	addr3	

This is so we can enter a very simple formula in B2:

| B2 | | | ▼ | ⋮ | ✕ | ✓ | *fx* | =IF(A1="",A2,B1) |

◢	A	B	C	D	E	F
1						
2	Jones, Jim	Jones, Jim				
3	addr1					
4	city1, State1 Zip1					
5						
6	Smith, Bill					
7	Addr2					
8	Addr2 part2					
9	City2, State2 Zip2					

The formula takes advantage of the blank between address-sets, hence the need to insert a row. It says that if the row above is empty, use the name (from A2), otherwise use the row above. Watch what happens when we fill this down: (*important – include one extra blank row at the bottom to keep the separation between addresses when we sort*)

| B2 | | | ▾ | ⋮ | × | ✓ | fx | =IF(A1="",A2,B1) |

◢	A	B	C	D	E	F
1						
2	Jones, Jim	Jones, Jim				
3	addr1	Jones, Jim				
4	city1, State1 Zip1	Jones, Jim				
5		Jones, Jim				
6	Smith, Bill	Smith, Bill				
7	Addr2	Smith, Bill				
8	Addr2 part2	Smith, Bill				
9	City2, State2 Zip2	Smith, Bill				
10	emailaddr	Smith, Bill				
11		Smith, Bill				
12	Johnson, Alice	Johnson, Alice				
13	addr3	Johnson, Alice				
14	Cityt3, State3 Zip3	Johnson, Alice				
15	email1	Johnson, Alice				

Why, now we have a field to sort on!

	A	B	C	D	E	F	G
1							
2	Jones, Jim	Jones, Jim					
3	addr1	Jones, Jim					
4	city1, State1 Zip1	Jones, Jim					
5		Jones, Jim					
6	Smith, Bill	Smith, Bill					
7	Addr2	Smith, Bill					
8	Addr2 part2	Smith, Bill					
9	City2, State2 Zip2	Smith, Bill					
10	emailaddr	Smith, Bill					

Sort

+ Add Level   × Delete Level   📋 Copy Level

Column		Sort On
Sort by	Column B ⌄	Cell Values

Since there *may* be a #REF! error after the sort, it's best to copy/paste special values first!

...resulting in:

	A	B	C
1			
2	Bergman, Sylvia	Bergman, Sylvia	
3	addr5	Bergman, Sylvia	
4	City5, State5 Zip5	Bergman, Sylvia	
5		Bergman, Sylvia	
6	Johnson, Alice	Johnson, Alice	
7	addr3	Johnson, Alice	
8	Cityt3, State3 Zip3	Johnson, Alice	
9	email1	Johnson, Alice	
10	email2	Johnson, Alice	
11	POBox 3333	Johnson, Alice	
12		Johnson, Alice	
13	Jones, Jim	Jones, Jim	
14	addr1	Jones, Jim	
15	city1, State1 Zip1	Jones, Jim	
16		Jones, Jim	
17	Smith, Bill	Smith, Bill	

All there is left to do is clear column B!

Mailing Label tricks - 3

Suppose you have data in column A like the following, and you want to rearrange it to look like C:E:

◢	A	B	C	D	E
1	Name1		Name1	address1	City, State Zip1
2	address1		Craig	address2	City, State Zip2
3	City, State Zip1				
4					
5	Craig				
6	address2				
7	City, State Zip2				
8					
9	Bob				
10	address3				
11	City, State Zip3				
12					
13	Mary				
14	address4				
15	City, State Zip4				

You might try entering a few references in C1:E2 like this:

◢	A	B	C	D	E
1	Name1		=A1	=A2	=A3
2	address1		=A5	=A6	=A7
3	City, State Zip1				
4					
5	Craig				
6	address2				
7	City, State Zip2				
8					
9	Bob				

…and then select C1:E2 and use the fill handle to drag down:

C	D	E
=A1	=A2	=A3
=A5	=A6	=A7
=A3	=A4	=A5
=A7	=A8	=A9
=A5	=A6	=A7
=A9	=A10	=A11
=A7	=A8	=A9
=A11	=A12	=A13

Clearly not what you want!! That looks like this:

C	D	E
Name1	address1	City, State Zip1
Craig	address2	City, State Zip2
City, State Zip1		0 Craig
City, State Zip2		0 Bob
Craig	address2	City, State Zip2
Bob	address3	City, State Zip3
Cit... Ctot. 7in2		0 Doh

No no no!

So how do you do it? Enter this text (no formulas):

C	D	E
xA1	xA2	xA3
xA5	xA6	xA7

Hang on – it'll get clearer…

Now select C1:E2 and fill down with the fill handle:

C	D	E
xA1	xA2	xA3
xA5	xA6	xA7
xA9	xA10	xA11
xA13	xA14	xA15
xA17	xA18	xA19

Yes! So now replace x with =:

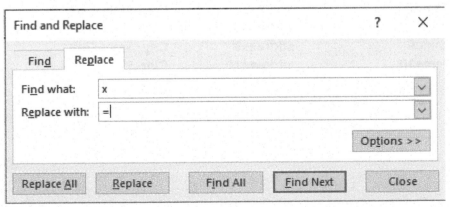

Click Replace All:

C	D	E
Name1	address1	City, State Zip1
Craig	address2	City, State Zip2
Bob	address3	City, State Zip3
Mary	address4	City, State Zip4
Mark	address5	City, State Zip5
Name6	address6	City, State Zip6
Name7	address7	City, State Zip7
Name8	address8	City, State Zip8
Name9	address9	City, State Zip9

Here's another approach:

This particular set of data went to row 160. Enter this in C1:

=INDEX(A:A,SEQUENCE(160/4,4))

--Of course you could have entered =INDEX(A:A,SEQUENCE(40,4))

And you'll see:

✕ ✓ fx	=INDEX(A:A,SEQUENCE(160/4,4))	

C	D	E
Name1	address1	City, State Zip1
Craig	address2	City, State Zip2
Bob	address3	City, State Zip3
Mary	address4	City, State Zip4
Mark	address5	City, State Zip5
Name6	address6	City, State Zip6
Name7	address7	City, State Zip7
Name8	address8	City, State Zip8
Name9	address9	City, State Zip9
Name10	address10	City, State Zip10

Ensuring users don't open your workbook with the shift key down to prevent your macros from kicking in!

Here's a simple technique to ensure they allow your macros to run. Save the workbook with only one sheet showing, and that sheet may look like this:

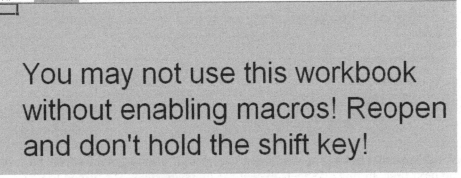

Prevent them from unhiding any other sheets by protecting the workbook's structure with a password. Use Review/Protect Workbook:

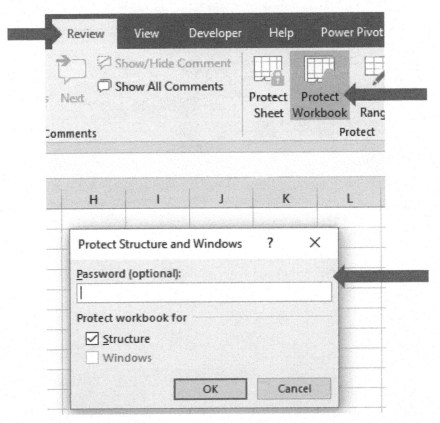

Then supply a password:

Your Workbook_Open event procedure or Auto_Open procedure has the code to hide the message sheet and unhide the other sheets by unprotecting the workbook and supplying the password:

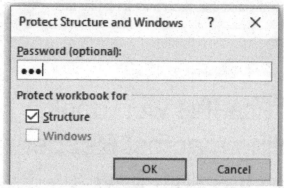

Notice also that before the workbook is closed, it also resets the sheets back for the next time, hiding all sheets except the message sheet. It's turned to visible first because you can't hide *all* the sheets in a workbook!

Lastly, you can protect access to the VBA code by using this in the VBE:

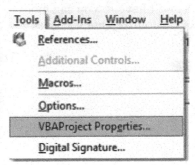

And then:

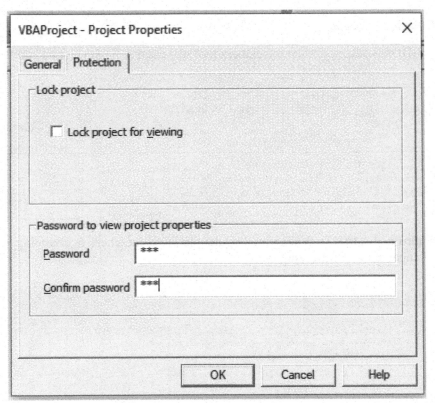

So now, if the user opens the workbook with the shift key down, it's a fairly useless workbook!

Oddities with the Camera Tool

The first image is created by the camera tool (if you don't have it, you can modify the QAT by right-clicking on the QAT and select Customize Quick Access Toolbar and search for Camera Tool.

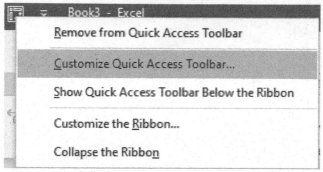

Range A1:G10 was selected, then the camera tool was used and "developed" on cell H2:

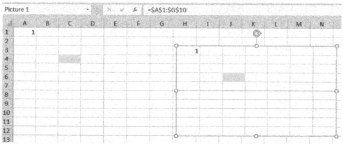

You see a mirror of A1:G10. When you drag the picture somewhere overlapping A1:G10, you get another mirroring effect:

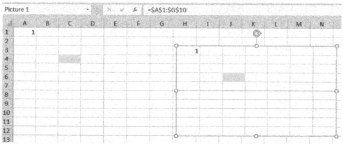

Bring it still closer:

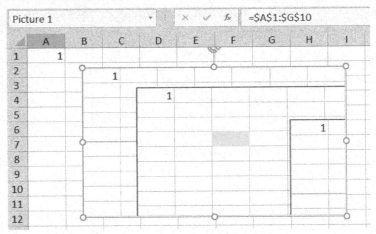

And still closer:

Now, change the value in cell A1 (from 1 to 2). Note that the first image only picks up the 2:

Now, change the value in cell A1 to a 3. Note that the first image only picks up the 3, *but the 2 and previous 1's are still there!*:

	A	B	C	D	E	F	G	H
1	3							
2			3					
3				2				
4					1			
5					1			
6							1	
7								
8								
9								
10								
11								

Where are they actually being stored?? Strange!

Another Camera Tool oddity:

In the following illustration, range A1:C12 was selected, the camera tool was clicked, and the picture was "developed" in range E1.

Picture 1			▾ ⋮ ✕ ✓ *fx*	=$A$1:$C$12		
	A	B	C	D	E	F	G
1	info	info	info		info	info	info
2	info	info	info		info	info	info
3	info	info	info		info	info	info
4	info	info	info		info	info	info
5	info	info	info		info	info	info
6	info	info	info		info	info	info
7	info	info	info		info	info	info
8	info	info	info		info	info	info
9	info	info	info		info	info	info
10	info	info	info		info	info	info
11	info	info	info		info	info	info
12	info	info	info		info	info	info

If you were to format this picture and give it no line and no fill (Ctrl/1), it would look like this:

However, the oddity is that even with no line and no fill, you can't select the cells underneath the picture, directly. It's being treated as if the picture *did* have a fill. You can *get to* the cells underneath (by F5 for Go To, or select a cell outside the picture area and move the arrows), as shown here (cell F6 was entered, and a bunch of dashes were typed):

E	F	G
info	info	info
info	info	info
info	info	info
info	info	info
info	info	info
info	~~info~~	info
info	info	info
info	info	info

Getting at the formatting of a cell to determine the sign

Look at this worksheet:

	✗ ✓ *fx*	123
D	**E**	
123.00 cr	-123	
44.00 db	44	
15.00 cr	-15	
123.44 db	123.44	
66.70 cr	-66.7	
14.00 db	14	
1.03 cr	-1.03	
122.00 db	122	
123.00 cr	-123	
55.00 db	55	

You can tell from the formula bar that the "cr" in cell D1 is via formatting only. The same is true for all values in column D. How can you change them to what you see in column E?

There's a formula in E1 and it is filled down:

=IF(RIGHT(fmt,2)="cr",-1,1)*D1

This is examining a range name, fmt, for the "cr" and returns -1 if found or -1 if not, then multiplies that by D1. So, the magic is in the name. The definition of fmt is

=GET.CELL(53,!D1)

But this was defined *while the cursor was in cell E1*, so fmt only works on the cell to the left. !D1 is a reference to the cell to the left which is applicable to all sheets in the workbook because the leading ! makes Excel not append the sheet name. GET.CELL(53) is a leftover function from XL4 macros and picks up the formatting of the cell referenced. Actually, the definition is

53 Contents of the cell as it is currently displayed, as text, including any additional numbers or symbols resulting from the cell's formatting.

You can see all these, not just 53, from the website:

https://www.mrexcel.com/board/threads/info-only-get-cell-arguments.20611/

A piece of silliness:

RE	RF	RG	RH
		What food is this?	

Answer: calamari. (Column RE)! (groan!)

DYNAMIC ARRAYS

Amazing Dynamic Array to list all files in a folder

This tips actually came to me in a dream! Really. I had to wake up to try it out, and, of course, it worked! Look at this worksheet:

	A	B	C
1	All files in current folder	Excel Files	Tab Names
2	=Fl	=FLx	=TabNames
3			

For now, each item in row 2 is preceded by an apostrophe. We'll examine them 1 at a time. If I remove the leading apostrophe in A2 and press enter…

	A	B
1	All files in current folder	Excel Files
2	0EAF6210.	=FLx
3	10 hour PT course.xlsm	
4	123.xlsx	
5	2007 Office Service Pack 2 Changes .xlsx	
6	293817.xlsx	
7	5.xlsx	
8	a.xlsx	
9	Accounts.xlsm	
10	acdc music.xlsm	
11	ACDC.wav	
12	ae.xls	
13	AllExperts Q&A.xls	
14	AllImages.xlsm	
15	API.pdf	
16	BarMitzvah.xls	

It's getting *all* the files in the current folder! Not just Excel files (note cell A11 or A15). Wow!

Putting the quote back and removing it from B2 gives us just Excel files: Another wow!

B	C
Excel Files	Tab Names
10 hour PT course.xlsm	=TabNames
123.xlsx	
2007 Office Service Pack 2 Changes .xlsx	
293817.xlsx	
5.xlsx	
a.xlsx	
Accounts.xlsm	
acdc music.xlsm	
ae.xls	
AllExperts Q&A.xls	
AllImages.xlsm	

Lastly, putting the quote back and removing it from C2 and we get the tab names. And sorted!:

C
Tab Names
1st and 15th
39%
3x3 Grid
Add Time
Amazing Formula
Conditional Formatting
Distribute
Dynamic Array Magic
Enter Totals
Files etc
Filter magic

How was this done??

In Excel 4, yes 4, there was a macro language called XLM which is still available. One of the commands was =FILES() which produced a list of all the files in the current directory. Here's a snippet of XLM code:

	A
1	=FILES()
2	=RETURN()

If I press ctrl/~ to see the values rather than formulas, I see

	A
1	0EAF6210.
2	FALSE

What's this? Here's a repeat screenshot from before:

	A	
1	All files in current folder	Exc
2	0EAF6210.	=FI
3	10 hour PT course.xlsm	
4	123.xlsx	
5	2007 Office Service Pack 2 Change	

Notice cell A2 is the same. (Whatever 0EAF6210. is!)

If I use F9 to evaluate =FILES() in the formula bar, I'd see this:

```
={"0EAF6210.","10 hour PT course.xlsm","123.xlsx","2007 Office Service Pack 2 Changes .xlsx","293817.xlsx","5.xlsx","a.xlsx","Accounts.xlsm","acdc
music.xlsm","ACDC.wav","ae.xls","AllExperts Q&A.xls","AllImages.xlsm","API.pdf","BarMitzvah.xls","Baseball-Softball_Hitting_&
_Pitching_Stat_Sheet_65_Game_Ver_with_charts VB65H-Beta single game stats.xls","Baseball-Softball_Hitting_&_Pitching_Stat_Sheet_65
_Game_Ver_with_charts.xls","Baseball-Softball_Hitting_&_Pitching_Stat_Sheet_65_Game_Ver_with_charts.xlsm","Beat the Dealer card.xlsm",
```

Since I don't want to make this an Excel4 Macro lesson, suffice it to say that this is something I remember from the days I used XLM, before VBA (I've been using Excel since 1986!) and I recognized this as an array and dreamt that the new dynamic arrays might be able to know this.

=FILES() is not a valid Excel function, but when used as a defined name, it works. So, I tried it and saw this:

A1				▼	:	×	✓	fx	=FIrstAttempt		

	A	B	C	D	E	F	G	H	I	J
1	0EAF6210.	10 hour PT	123.xlsx	2007 Offic	293817.xls	5.xlsx	a.xlsx	Accounts.x	acdc music	ACDC.wav	ae
2										

Ah! I could use =TRANSPOSE(firstattempt):

	A	B	C	D	E	F	G

Formula bar: =TRANSPOSE(FIrstAttempt)

	A	B	C	D	E	F	G
	OEAF6210.						
	10 hour PT course.xlsm						
	123.xlsx						
	2007 Office Service Pack 2 Changes .xlsx						
	293817.xlsx						
	5.xlsx						
	a.xlsx						
	Accounts.xlsm						
	acdc music.xlsm						

YES! But why not put the TRANSPOSE in the defined name?

OK, here's the definitions of Fl, Flx, and TABNAMES:

Fl	=TRANSPOSE(FILES())
Flx	=TRANSPOSE(FILES("*.xl*"))
TabNames	=SORT(TRANSPOSE(MID(GET.WORKBOOK(1),FIND("]",GET.WORKBOOK(1))+1,255)))

So Flx filters the FILES by putting in wildcards around .xl to limit the files to Excel files --FILES("*.xl*").

TabNames uses an old XLM statement of GET.WORKBOOK(1). If I only used a defined name (I used "gw") as TRANSPOSE(Get.WORKBOOK(1)), I'd see this:

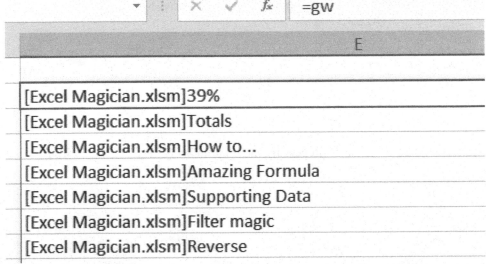

Formula bar: =gw

	E
	[Excel Magician.xlsm]39%
	[Excel Magician.xlsm]Totals
	[Excel Magician.xlsm]How to...
	[Excel Magician.xlsm]Amazing Formula
	[Excel Magician.xlsm]Supporting Data
	[Excel Magician.xlsm]Filter magic
	[Excel Magician.xlsm]Reverse

This includes the name of the workbook before the tab name, so the formula is more complex to weed out the characters after the "]". Then, after transposing, it's passed to the SORT function.

Getting an NxN grid of non-repeating integers

For this example, I'll use 3x3. As you can see, the values in A3:D5 are integers 1-9 and they don't repeat. With every calculation, this refreshes with a different sequence. How?

	A	B	C	D	E
1	Want 3x3 grid of non-repeating random integers 1-9				
2					
3	5	1	4		
4	7	8	2		
5	3	9	6		

Let's look at how I approached this. First, I did a SEQUENCE(9) to get the integers, then next to it I used a RANDARRAY(9) to get:

=RANDARRAY(9)

G	H
1	0.60932
2	0.536122
3	0.264909
4	0.786475
5	0.062997
6	0.635793
7	0.773702
8	0.803323
9	0.899836

Next, I wanted to sort the integers by the random array and came up with the SORTBY:

=SORTBY(SEQUENCE(9),RANDARRAY(9))

J	K	L	M
5			
7			
3			
2			
4			
8			
9			
6			
1			

If I use INDEX to get at any of these numbers, I'll get one and I need all of them -- and in a 3x3 grid somehow.

I tried something I didn't think would work, but it did:

=INDEX(SORTBY(SEQUENCE(9),RANDARRAY(9)),SEQUENCE(3,3))

E	F	G	H	I	J
6	7	1			
4	9	8			
3	5	2			

Reversing a string
Look at this worksheet:

	A	B
1	Hello	olleH
2	Very cool!	!looc yreV
3	Madam I'm Adam	madA m'I madaM
4	Able was I ere I saw Elba	ablE was I ere I saw elbA
5	A man a plan a canal Panama	amanaP lanac a nalp a nam A

As you can see, Column B is simply the reverse of column A. The formula in B1 is =TEXTJOIN("",,MID(A1,SEQUENCE(LEN(A1),1,LEN(A1),-1),1))

Let me explain. LEN(A1) is 5. So, SEQUENCE(LEN(A1)) is SEQUENCE(5), which is 1;2;3;4;5.

The part that is SEQUENCE(LEN(A1),1,LEN(A1),-1) is 5;4;3;2;1. That's because the 3rd parameter in the SEQUENCE function is the starting value, and the -1 is the step by. So, this is SEQUENCE(5,1,5,-1) which is the reverse of SEQUENCE(5). The MID(A1,SEQUENCE(LEN(A1),1,LEN(A1),-1),1) part is now MID(A1,{5;4;3;2;1},1) which is {"o";"l";"l";"e";"H"}.

The TEXTJOIN is using a delimiter of "", or null, so it puts them all together.

Filter Magic

Here's a sample data set, in a table:

	A	B	C	D	E	F	G	H	I	J	K
1	Region	Market	State	Customer Name	Account Manager	Order Date	Ship Date	Product Category	Quantity	Sale Amount	Equipment Cost
2	Southeast	Charlotte	NC	BYPOS Corp.	Aida Carden	07/01/06	07/08/06	Concession Equipment	6	$4,998	$4,250
3	South	Florida	FL	STOHLM Corp.	Ashleigh Friedman	07/01/06	07/08/06	Fryers	1	$13	$3
4	CANADA	CANADA	ON	LUUDST Corp.	Jarvis Mcdonough	07/01/06	07/08/06	Refrigerators and Coolers	1	$4,637	$2,356
5	Southeast	Charlotte	NC	BYPOS Corp.	Aida Carden	07/01/06	07/08/06	Warmers	1	$822	$694
6	West	California	CA	COMPPU Corp.	Dustin Gamboa	07/05/06	07/12/06	Commercial Appliances	1	$829	$553
7	Northeast	Buffalo	NY	BLWHU Corp.	Martin Stamps	07/22/06	07/29/06	Refrigerators and Coolers	1	$4,637	$2,356

This data continues for over 1000 rows.

Using the FILTER function, we can filter by *two* criteria, Region and State:

M6 = `=FILTER(Magic,(Magic[Region]=M2)*(Magic[State]=N2))`

	M	N	O	P	Q	R	S	T	U	V	W
1	Region	State									
2	Southwest	UT									
3											
4											
5	Region	Market	State	Customer Name	Account Manager	Order Date	Ship Date	Product Category	Quantity	Sale Amount	Equipment Cost
6	Southwest	Denver	UT	GUNCOM Corp.	Marlin Stubblefield	38954	38961	Refrigerators and Coolers	1	4637	2356.05
7	Southwest	Denver	UT	TUMBRU Corp.	Marlin Stubblefield	39470	39477	Ovens and Ranges	1	3578	1636.6787
8	Southwest	Denver	UT	UNVARU Corp.	Marlin Stubblefield	39638	39645	Fryers	1	13	2.9414
9	Southwest	Denver	UT	CRUATI Corp.	Marlin Stubblefield	39711	39718	Refrigerators and Coolers	1	4120	2021.4959
10	Southwest	Denver	UT	QWUTT Corp.	Marlin Stubblefield	39743	39750	Bar Equipment	1	20	4.4946
11	Southwest	Denver	UT	MTNHA Corp.	Marlin Stubblefield	39776	39783	Fryers	1	53	13.325
12	Southwest	Denver	UT	DIRANC Corp.	Marlin Stubblefield	39782	39789	Bar Equipment	1	6	1.2738

The name of the table is "Magic", and the formula in M6 is
=FILTER(Magic,(Magic[Region]=M2)*(Magic[State]=N2)).

The titles in row 5 were manually entered (well, copied and pasted), but to get
the two criteria, we need to multiply arguments in the "Include" part of the Filter
function to simulate an AND condition. (You use + to simulate an OR condition).
So here, we filtered for a region of Southwest and a State of UT. This is nothing
new.

A trick I learned from MVP Leila Gharani was to pick and choose the columns
you want to display:

Y6 = `=FILTER(FILTER(Magic,(Magic[Region]=Y2)*(Magic[State]=Z2)),{1,0,1,0,1,0,1,0,0,0,0})`

	Y	Z	AA	AB	AC	AD	AE	AF	AG	AH	AI	AJ
1	Region	State										
2	Southwest	UT										
3												
4												
5	Region	State	Account Manager	Ship Date								
6	Southwest	UT	Marlin Stubblefield	9/1/2006								
7	Southwest	UT	Marlin Stubblefield	1/30/2008								
8	Southwest	UT	Marlin Stubblefield	7/16/2008								
9	Southwest	UT	Marlin Stubblefield	9/27/2008								
10	Southwest	UT	Marlin Stubblefield	10/29/2008								
11	Southwest	UT	Marlin Stubblefield	12/1/2008								
12	Southwest	UT	Marlin Stubblefield	12/7/2008								

The formula in Y6 is =FILTER(FILTER(Magic,(Magic[Region]=Y2)*(Magic[St
ate]=Z2)),{1,0,1,0,1,0,1,0,0,0,0})

Yes, FILTER(FILTER...!

We're filtering the filtered result from before, and adding a new "Include" argument, which corresponds to the columns we want to show. This was entered as
an array constant, {1,0,1,0,1,0,1,0,0,0,0} – note the curly braces. Each 1 means

show the column. A 0 means do not show the column. There are 4 1's in that array constant, and 4 columns are showing as a result of the FILTER formula above.

Then I discovered my trick to be able to show the columns in the order I want! I added to Leila's trick and came up with this:

```
=SORTBY(FILTER(FILTER(Magic,(Magic[Region]=AM2)*(Magic[State]=AN2),""),{1,0,1,0,1,0,1,0,0,0,0}),{2,1,4,3})
```

AM	AN	AO	AP	AQ	AR	AS	AT	AU
Region	State							
Southwest	UT							

State	Region	Ship Date	Account Manager					
UT	Southwest	9/1/2006	Marlin Stubblefield					
UT	Southwest	1/30/2008	Marlin Stubblefield					
UT	Southwest	7/16/2008	Marlin Stubblefield					
UT	Southwest	9/27/2008	Marlin Stubblefield					
UT	Southwest	10/29/2008	Marlin Stubblefield					
UT	Southwest	12/1/2008	Marlin Stubblefield					
UT	Southwest	12/7/2008	Marlin Stubblefield					
UT	Southwest	1/3/2009	Marlin Stubblefield					

I surrounded that FILTER(FILTER… with a SORTBY! The formula in cell AM5 is =SORTBY(FILTER(FILTER(Magic,(Magic[Region]=AM2)*(Magic[State]= AN2),""),{1,0,1,0,1,0,1,0,0,0,0}),{2,1,4,3})

The new piece is SORTBY(…,{2,1,4,3}). This sorts the FILTER(FILTER from above and puts the 2nd column first, then the first column, then the 4th, and finally the 3rd. Cool stuff!

More Filter Magic - Adding a Total Row
This idea came from Jon Acampora, Microsoft MVP.

Here's part of a table that's used in this example:

	A	B	C	D	E	F
1	Agent	Date Listed	Area	Amount	#Unit	Total
2	Adams	10/9/2007	Central	$53	15	$795
3	Adams	8/19/2007	Central	$18	1	$18
4	Adams	4/28/2007	Central	$38	4	$152
5	Adams	7/19/2007	Central	$133	11	$1,463
6	Adams	2/6/2007	Central	$27	4	$108
7	Adams	8/1/2007	Central	$109	2	$218
8	Adams	1/15/2007	Central	$16	13	$208
9	Jenkins	1/29/2007	N. County	$44	19	$836
10	Romero	4/4/2007	N. County	$8	15	$120
11	Hamilton	2/24/2007	N. County	$57	3	$171
12	Randolph	4/24/2007	N. County	$126	3	$378
13	Adams	4/21/2007	S. County	$76	4	$304
14	Shasta	3/24/2007	N. County	$87	17	$1,479
15	Kelly	6/9/2007	N. County	$48	2	$96

Further to the right is where the magic is shown. When I enter Adams in cell U1, I get a Filtered list of all the Adams in column Q plus a total at the bottom:

Q	R	S	T	U	V
				Adams	
Adams	10/9/2007	Central	53	15	795
Adams	8/19/2007	Central	18	1	18
Adams	4/28/2007	Central	38	4	152
Adams	7/19/2007	Central	133	11	1463
Adams	2/6/2007	Central	27	4	108
Adams	8/1/2007	Central	109	2	218
Adams	1/15/2007	Central	16	13	208
Adams	4/21/2007	S. County	76	4	304
Adams	6/6/2007	N. County	60	1	60
Adams	2/8/2007	N. County	60	5	300
Adams	5/24/2007	N. County	76	4	304
Adams	4/15/2007	N. County	46	18	828
Total					4,758

If I change Adams to Romero, I get a different list, *but the Total row has moved up* against the bottom of the list. How was this done?

Q	R	S	T	U	V	W
				Romero		
Romero	4/4/2007	N. County	8	15	120	
Romero	1/28/2007	N. County	90	3	270	
Romero	8/3/2007	N. County	147	5	735	
Romero	3/16/2007	Central	76	7	532	
Romero	5/1/2007	Central	57	14	798	
Romero	8/26/2007	S. County	71	10	710	
Romero	7/29/2007	N. County	100	7	700	
Total					3,865	

The formula in Q3 is =SORTBY(I3#:I2,H3#:H2), which is an odd formula in itself, since it references a spill range (I3#) through a cell *before* the spill range (I2). We'll examine this a bit later. (If I used I2:I3# -- reversing the order – I get a #REF! error!)

So, let's look at what's going on in column I (I through N was actually hidden so the magic really shows in Q:V):

f_x	=FILTER(Table13,Table13[Agent]=U1,"NO MATCH")

	I	J	K	L	M	N	O
13	Total					4758	
1	Adams	10/9/2007	Central	53	15	795	
2	Adams	8/19/2007	Central	18	1	18	
3	Adams	4/28/2007	Central	38	4	152	
4	Adams	7/19/2007	Central	133	11	1463	
5	Adams	2/6/2007	Central	27	4	108	
6	Adams	8/1/2007	Central	109	2	218	
7	Adams	1/15/2007	Central	16	13	208	
8	Adams	4/21/2007	S. County	76	4	304	
9	Adams	6/6/2007	N. County	60	1	60	
10	Adams	2/8/2007	N. County	60	5	300	
11	Adams	5/24/2007	N. County	76	4	304	
12	Adams	4/15/2007	N. County	46	18	828	

This formula is a straightforward FILTER formula, filtering the Table13 where the agent matches what's in cell U1 (Adams, Romero…). The formula in N2 is the total, =SUM(OFFSET(N3,0,0,10000,1)). Cell H3 contains =SEQUENCE(ROWS(I3#)) which produces the numbers 1 through 12 in this example, but for Romero it produces 1 through 7. Lastly, the number in H2 is simply =ROWS(I3#)+1 to get the next number in the sequence. This could have been the hard coded value of 10000 or something to force the sorting of range H2:N14 (in this case) to put the total line at the bottom.

Now back to cell Q3, =SORTBY(I3#:I2,H3#:H2). We don't want the numbers 1 through 13 to show in the result, so the SORTBY will sort the spill range of I3# *by* the spill range of H3#. But that would miss the total row, so we include it by the odd reference I3#:I2 and H3#:H2.

Thanks again to Jon Acampora.

Filtering as you type

In this trick I'll show how you can filter *as you type each letter in the criteria!*

Here's the worksheet I'll be using:

| J4 | | | × ✓ fx | =FILTER(Magic,ISNUMBER(SEARCH(M1,Magic[Product Category])),"Not Found") |

	I	J	K	L	M	N	O	P	Q	R
1		Product Category==>								
2										
3		Region	Market	State	Customer Name	Account Manager	Order Date	Ship Date	Product Category	
4		Southeast	Charlotte	NC	BYPOS Corp.	Alda Carden	7/1/2006	7/8/2006	Concession Equipment	
5		South	Florida	FL	STOHLM Corp.	Ashleigh Friedman	7/1/2006	7/8/2006	Fryers	
6		CANADA	CANADA	ON	LUUDST Corp.	Jarvis Mcdonough	7/1/2006	7/8/2006	Refrigerators and Coolers	
7		Southeast	Charlotte	NC	BYPOS Corp.	Alda Carden	7/1/2006	7/8/2006	Warmers	
8		West	California	CA	COMPPU Corp.	Dustin Gamboa	7/5/2006	7/12/2006	Commercial Appliances	
9		Northeast	Buffalo	NY	BLWHU Corp.	Martin Stamps	7/22/2006	7/29/2006	Refrigerators and Coolers	
10		South	Florida	FL	UMUSAL Corp.	Ashleigh Friedman	8/1/2006	8/8/2006	Concession Equipment	
11		South	Florida	FL	HUSZUG Corp.	Ashleigh Friedman	8/1/2006	8/8/2006	Fryers	
12		South	Florida	FL	SUASHW Corp.	Ashleigh Friedman	8/1/2006	8/8/2006	Ovens and Ranges	

The formula in cell J4 is:

=FILTER(Magic,ISNUMBER(SEARCH(M1,Magic[Product Category])),"Not Found")

As long as whatever is in cell M1 is found in the Product Category column of the "Magic" table, the filtering will happen just as if I typed directly into cell M1 and pressed enter, but for each character typed!

If what is typed *is* found, then the SEARCH (case *in*sensitive) will give a number and the ISNUMBER will return TRUE, so that record is one of the candidates for the FILTER function.

The table is named Magic and is the same table as we've seen before. Sitting on top of cells L1:M1 is an ActiveX Text Box that is linked to cell M1, so as I type in the text box, whatever is typed simultaneously shows up in cell M1, which affects the FILTER formula and therefore affects what's being shown, letter by letter. For example, if I type the letter "a", I see:

Product Category==>	a						
Region	Market	State	Customer Name	Account Manager	Order Date	Ship Date	Product Category
CANADA	CANADA	ON	LUUDST Corp.	Jarvis Mcdonough	7/1/2006	7/8/2006	Refrigerators and Coolers
Southeast	Charlotte	NC	BYPOS Corp.	Alda Carden	7/1/2006	7/8/2006	Warmers
West	California	CA	COMPPU Corp.	Dustin Gamboa	7/5/2006	7/12/2006	Commercial Appliances
Northeast	Buffalo	NY	BLWHU Corp.	Martin Stamps	7/22/2006	7/29/2006	Refrigerators and Coolers
South	Florida	FL	SUASHW Corp.	Ashleigh Friedman	8/1/2006	8/8/2006	Ovens and Ranges
South	Florida	FL	WHATLU Corp.	Ashleigh Friedman	8/1/2006	8/8/2006	Ovens and Ranges
South	Florida	GA	GLEAS Corp.	Tory Hanlon	8/1/2006	8/8/2006	Refrigerators and Coolers
South	Florida	FL	GRUGS Corp.	Ashleigh Friedman	8/21/2006	8/28/2006	Refrigerators and Coolers

You can see that what was shown in the previous illustration in cell Q4, "Concession Equipment" is not shown since there's no "a" in that text. If I continue to type an "n", so that the ActiveX box shows "an", I then see:

Product Category==> | an|

Region	Market	State	Customer Name	Account Manager	Order Date	Ship Date	Product Category
CANADA	CANADA	ON	LUUDST Corp.	Jarvis Mcdonough	7/1/2006	7/8/2006	Refrigerators and Coolers
West	California	CA	COMPPU Corp.	Dustin Gamboa	7/5/2006	7/12/2006	Commercial Appliances
Northeast	Buffalo	NY	BLWHU Corp.	Martin Stamps	7/22/2006	7/29/2006	Refrigerators and Coolers
South	Florida	FL	SUASHW Corp.	Ashleigh Friedman	8/1/2006	8/8/2006	Ovens and Ranges
South	Florida	FL	WHATLU Corp.	Ashleigh Friedman	8/1/2006	8/8/2006	Ovens and Ranges

and the list is shorter. Continuing, I now type "d":

and only those products with the word "and" are showing. If

Product Category==> | and|

Region	Market	State	Customer Name	Account Manager	Order Date	Ship Date	Product Category
CANADA	CANADA	ON	LUUDST Corp.	Jarvis Mcdonough	7/1/2006	7/8/2006	Refrigerators and Coolers
Northeast	Buffalo	NY	BLWHU Corp.	Martin Stamps	7/22/2006	7/29/2006	Refrigerators and Coolers
South	Florida	FL	SUASHW Corp.	Ashleigh Friedman	8/1/2006	8/8/2006	Ovens and Ranges
South	Florida	FL	WHATLU Corp.	Ashleigh Friedman	8/1/2006	8/8/2006	Ovens and Ranges
South	Florida	GA	GLEAS Corp.	Tory Hanlon	8/1/2006	8/8/2006	Refrigerators and Coolers

now type a space and R:

Product Category==> | and r|

Region	Market	State	Customer Name	Account Manager	Order Date	Ship Date	Product Category
South	Florida	FL	SUASHW Corp.	Ashleigh Friedman	8/1/2006	8/8/2006	Ovens and Ranges
South	Florida	FL	WHATLU Corp.	Ashleigh Friedman	8/1/2006	8/8/2006	Ovens and Ranges
Southeast	Charlotte	NC	MCDUWU Corp.	Alda Carden	9/1/2006	9/8/2006	Ovens and Ranges
South	Florida	FL	EARLAQ Corp.	Ashleigh Friedman	10/1/2006	10/8/2006	Ovens and Ranges
South	Florida	FL	FUSMAL Corp.	Ashleigh Friedman	10/1/2006	10/8/2006	Ovens and Ranges

You get the idea. If I had typed z to start:

Product Category==> | z|

Region	Market	State	Customer Name	Account Manager	Order Date	Ship Date	Product Category
Not Found							

then I get the error "Not Found" because there are no products with a z!

Let's get back to that ActiveX control and how it was created:

From the Developer tab, the Controls group, the Insert dropdown shows Form Controls and ActiveX Controls:

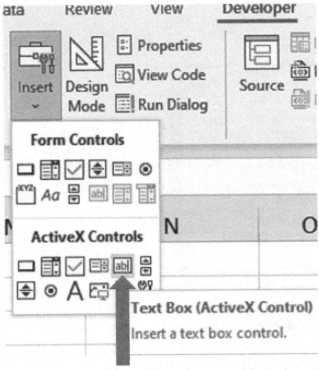

The red arrow points to the ActiveX Text Box. Once you click this, you draw the control onto the worksheet. That will put you into "Design mode":

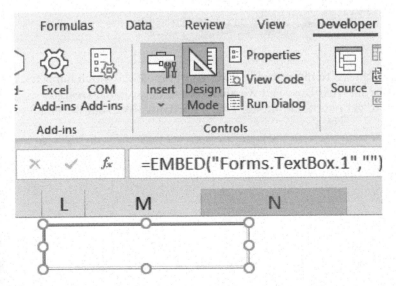

Right next to the Design mode is a Properties command, and when you click it you see:

Properties

TextBox2 TextBox	

Alphabetic | Categorized

(Name)	TextBox2
AutoLoad	False
AutoSize	False
AutoTab	False
AutoWordSelect	True
BackColor	&H80000005&
BackStyle	1 - fmBackStyleOpaque
BorderColor	&H80000006&
BorderStyle	0 - fmBorderStyleNone
DragBehavior	0 - fmDragBehaviorDisabled
Enabled	True
EnterFieldBehavior	0 - fmEnterFieldBehaviorSelectAll
EnterKeyBehavior	False
Font	Calibri
ForeColor	&H80000008&
Height	30.75
HideSelection	True
IMEMode	0 - fmIMEModeNoControl
IntegralHeight	True
Left	794.25
LinkedCell	
Locked	True
MaxLength	0

The LinkedCell is what we're interested in here, and I typed M1 which happens to also be covered by the Text Box. But we also have to click on the Design Mode button again to get out of that mode. That's fairly involved, but the effect is great!

Create a hyperlinked, sorted Table of Contents of all sheets

First, I will demo it, then show the formula that does the trick. Here's a screen-shot:

f_x	=ShtsSorted

	E	F	G	H	I	J
	=HYPERLINK("[Excel Magician.xlsm]'1st and 15th'!A1")					
	=HYPERLINK("[Excel Magician.xlsm]'39%'!A1")					
	=HYPERLINK("[Excel Magician.xlsm]'3x3 Grid'!A1")					
	=HYPERLINK("[Excel Magician.xlsm]'Add Time'!A1")					
	=HYPERLINK("[Excel Magician.xlsm]'Amazing Formula'!A1")					
	=HYPERLINK("[Excel Magician.xlsm]'Conditional Formatting'!A1")					
	=HYPERLINK("[Excel Magician.xlsm]'Distribute'!A1")					
	=HYPERLINK("[Excel Magician.xlsm]'Dynamic Array Magic'!A1")					
	=HYPERLINK("[Excel Magician.xlsm]'Enter Totals'!A1")					
	=HYPERLINK("[Excel Magician.xlsm]'Files etc'!A1")					
	=HYPERLINK("[Excel Magician.xlsm]'Filter magic'!A1")					
	=HYPERLINK("[Excel Magician.xlsm]'History '!A1")					
	=HYPERLINK("[Excel Magician.xlsm]'How to...'!A1")					

Cell E1 has a single dynamic array formula called ShtsSorted. It spilled into all the cells below that you see. The formula really only exists in cell E1. To make it work, we have to make the formulas in the spilled range be their own formulas and not part of a spilled range.

To do that, select the entire column E, copy, and paste special *values* on top of itself:

=HYPERLINK("[Excel Magician.xlsm]'1st and 15th'!A1")

E	F	G	H	I	J
=HYPERLINK("[Excel Magician.xlsm]'1st and 15th'!A1")					
=HYPERLINK("[Excel Magician.xlsm]'39%'!A1")					
=HYPERLINK("[Excel Magician.xlsm]'3x3 Grid'!A1")					
=HYPERLINK("[Excel Magician.xlsm]'Add Time'!A1")					
=HYPERLINK("[Excel Magician.xlsm]'Amazing Formula'!A1")					
=HYPERLINK("[Excel Magician.xlsm]'Conditional Formatting'!A1")					
=HYPERLINK("[Excel Magician.xlsm]'Distribute'!A1")					

You can tell from the Formula bar, it's now a Hyperlink, not =ShtsSorted. But these are not "real" formulas yet. You have to replace = with = to convert them:

The formula bar and cell E1 are now "different":

| *fx* | =HYPERLINK("[Excel Magician.xlsm]'1st and 15th'!A1") |

E	F	G	H	I
[Excel Magician.xlsm]'1st and 15th'!A1				
[Excel Magician.xlsm]'39%'!A1				
[Excel Magician.xlsm]'3x3 Grid'!A1				
[Excel Magician.xlsm]'Add Time'!A1				
[Excel Magician.xlsm]'Amazing Formula'!A1				
[Excel Magician.xlsm]'Conditional Formatting'!A1				

These are all now true hyperlinks, and if I hover over any of these, I see the hand cursor indicating a hyperlink, then it will take me to that tab when I click it, and cell A1. Once at A1 of the sheet you hyperlinked to, you can press Alt/Left-arrow to return to this sheet (probably should be named Table of Contents!)

OK, so what is the definition of ShtsSorted?

="=HYPERLINK("""""&SORT(TRANSPOSE(SUBSTITUTE(
GET.WORKBOOK(1),"]","]'")))&"'!A1""")"

First, notice it's *text.* ="=HYPERLINK(""""" starts a string which will become =HYPERLINK(". This is why we had to replace the = with = -- it was only a *string,* not a real formula. The SUBSTITUTE is adding a single quote to the "]", making it "]'" because if you look at the cell E1 above (repeated here for convenience):

| [Excel Magician.xlsm]'1st and 15th'!A1 |

there's a single quote after the] as well as before the ! which is the last part of the formula definition above – note it ends in &"'!A1""")" – hard to see, but there's a single quote inside the double quote.

Again, this is transposed so it's vertical, and passed to the SORT dynamic array function!

VBA

You can easily get to your VBA routine from the Excel sheet by using F5 (Go To) and typing the routine name:

If you have a routine named Tabs, you can get to it directly (it won't show up as a named range, so you have to type it in):

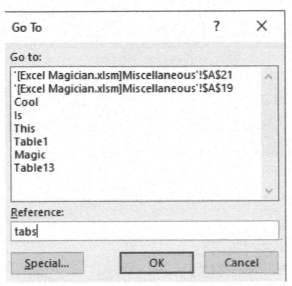

And here's the result:

```vba
Sub Tabs()
    For i = 1 To Worksheets.Count
        Cells(i, 1).Value = Worksheets(i).Name
    Next
End Sub
```

Using R1C1 to copy an involved formula to use in your VBA routine

Suppose you have a long or involved formula such as this in your worksheet:

=IF(OR(F84<>H84,F235<>H235,F386<>H386,F537<>H537,
F688<>H688,F839<>H839,F990<>H990,F1141<>H1141,
F1292<>H1292,F1443<>H1443,F1594<>H1594,F1745<>H1745,
F4161<>H4161),T1,"")

And you need to be able to *create* this formula from VBA code, inside a
Range(whatever).FormulaR1C1=??

You can temporarily change to R1C1 notation by File/Options/Formulas:

xcel Options

General	
Formulas	⊞▯fx Change options related to formula calcula
Data	**Calculation options**
Proofing	Workbook Calculation ⓘ
Save	◯ A̲utomatic
	◯ Automatic except for d̲ata tables
Language	◉ M̲anual
Ease of Access	☐ Recalculate w̲orkbook before saving
Advanced	**Working with formulas**
Customize Ribbon	
Quick Access Toolbar	☑ R1C1 reference style ⓘ ◀━━━
	☑ Formula AutoComplete ⓘ

=IF(OR(R[83]C[-21]<>R[83]C[-19],R[234]C[-21]<>R[234]C[-19],R[385]
C[-21]<>R[385]C[-19],R[536]C[-21]<>R[536]C[-19],R[687]C[-21]<>R[687]
C[-19],R[838]C[-21]<>R[838]C[-19],R[989]C[-21]<>R[989]C[-19],R[1140]C[-
21]<>R[1140]C[-19],R[1291]C[-21]<>R[1291]C[-19],R[1442]C[-21]<>R[1442]
C[-19],R[1593]C[-21]<>R[1593]C[-19],R[1744]C[-21]<>R[1744]C[-
19],R[4160]C[-21]<>R[4160]C[-19]),RC[-7],")

Then you can copy this formula and paste it into the FormulaR1C1, remembering
to double up on any "quotes. And when done, return to A1 notation by visiting
File/Options/Formulas again and *de*selecting the R1C1 reference style. The VBA
would then be:

Range(whatever).FormulaR1C1= "=IF(OR(R[83]C[-21]<>R[83]C[-19],R[234]
C[-21]<>R[234]C[-19],R[385]C[-21]<>R[385]C[-19],R[536]C[-21]<>R[536]
C[-19],R[687]C[-21]<>R[687]C[-19],R[838]C[-21]<>R[838]C[-19],R[989]
C[-21]<>R[989]C[-19],R[1140]C[-21]<>R[1140]C[-19],R[1291]C[-
21]<>R[1291]C[-19],R[1442]C[-21]<>R[1442]C[-19],R[1593]C[-21]<>R[1593]

C[-19],R[1744]C[-21]<>R[1744]C[-19],R[4160]C[-21]<>R[4160]C[-19]),RC[-7],"""")"

(Note the """" near the end, representing "" in the formula!)

Here is an alternative method that does not require switching to R1C1 reference style: Select the cell with the complicated formula. Alt/F11 to switch to VBA. Ctrl/G to open the Immediate window. Type the following and press Enter:

? ActiveCell.FormulaR1C1

The R1C1 version of the formula will appear in the Immedate window. Copy it, change " to "".

```
Immediate

? ActiveCell.FormulaR1C1
=IF(OR(R[82]C[2]<>R[82]C[4],R[233]C[2]<>R[23
R[686]C[2]<>R[686]C[4],R[837]C[2]<>R[837]C[4
R[1290]C[2]<>R[1290]C[4],R[1441]C[2]<>R[1441
R[4159]C[2]<>R[4159]C[4]),R[-1]C[16],"")
```

A VBA Shortcuts to select from a list

Suppose you have a variable defined as this:

Dim sav StringForHoldingTheDescription As String

...and you wanted to use it, obviously, later in your code. You can simply *start* typing it, then press Ctrl/Spacebar, which will give you this:

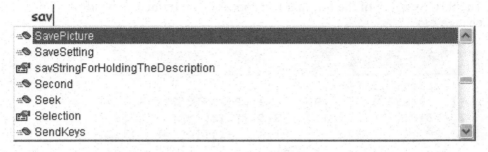

...and you can use the down arrow to select it, then the tab key (or enter key) to put in into your code:

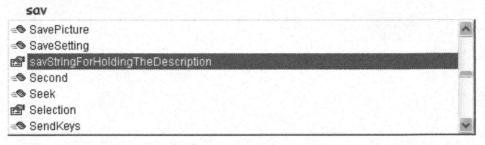

If what you typed is unique enough so there's really no choice (like if you typed "savs" then pressed Ctrl/Spacebar), Excel will simply put the entire variable right into the module.

As a matter of fact, it's not just for variables. How often do you type out Application? Simply typing Appl and pressing ctrl/spacebar will put Application right in the code!

"App" isn't quite enough for uniqueness:

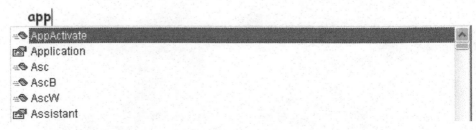

And, if you have *nothing* on the line and press ctrl/spacebar, you will still get the beginning of the list:

More VBA Keyboard Shortcuts

Alt/Q will bring you from the VBE to Excel. However, Alt/F11 is a toggle back and forth from/to VBE and Excel, so I prefer that one!

Ctrl/G will bring up the Immediate Pane.

If the cursor is *in* the immediate window, then Ctrl/A and then backspace will clear it.

If you right-click on a variable, you will see a dropdown where you can request the definition. This takes you to the DIM statement for that variable if it exists.

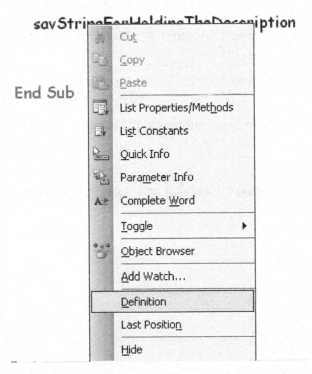

VBA Shortcut to fill ranges

Suppose you need to fill cells A1:D1 (using VBA) so it looks like this:

	A	B	C	D
1	Name	Account #	Date	Amount
2				

Most folk's VBA would look something like this:

```
Sub FillRange()
    Range("A1").Value = "Name"
    Range("B1").Value = "Account #"
    Range("C1").Value = "Date"
    Range("D1").Value = "Amount"
End Sub
```

...and that would work fine. But look at this version:

```
Sub FillRange()
    Range("A1:D1").Value = Array("Name", "Account #", "Date", "Amount")
End Sub
```

Not only is this shorter, but if the code needed to fill range A1:Z1, there'd be a *lot* less typing!

What if you wanted to fill A1:A4 with the same information? You might now be inclined to use this:

```
Sub FillRange()
    Range("A1:A4").Value = Array("Name", "Account #", "Date", "Amount")
End Sub
```

But that would surprisingly result in:

	A	B	C	D
1	Name			
2	Name			
3	Name			
4	Name			
5				

...not what you expect! You need to use this code to accomplish the vertical arrangement of the data:

```
Sub FillRange()
    Range("A1:A4").Value = Application.Transpose(Array("Name", "Account #", "Date", "Amount"))
End Sub
```

That is, you need to *transpose* the information. Since Transpose is a worksheet function, you need to use any of these combinations:

```
Application.Transpose
Application.WorksheetFunction.Transpose
WorksheetFunction.Transpose
```

The latter two will give the intellisense dropdown:

```
WorksheetFunction.
```

The reason I chose the first one (without the intellisense) is that it's the shortest amount of typing!!

VBA Boolean test

Instead of using this to turn a Boolean variable to True/False:

```
Sub BooleanTest()
Dim MyBool As Boolean
    If Range("A12").Value > 12 Then
        MyBool = True
    Else
        MyBool = False
    End If
End Sub
```

You can use this to do the same thing:

```
Sub BooleanTest()
Dim MyBool As Boolean
    MyBool = (Range("A12").Value > 12)
End Sub
```

The expression (Range("A12").Value > 12) will be evaluated and if it *is* greater than 12, MyBool will be set to True, else it will be set to False, the same as in the first example! Quite a bit shorter!

Multi-select offset

Did you ever have an odd selection and wanted to have the same selection 2 columns over (or 1 or a few rows down, etc.) to repeat some action? Here's an oddly shaped selection, all filled with 123:

	A	B	C	D
1		123		
2		123		
3			123	
4			123	
5		123		
6				123
7			123	
8			123	
9			123	
10			123	
11		123		
12		123		
13		123		
14			123	
15				

Now you want the same shape beginning in D1. The easiest way to do it is using the VBE's immediate window to execute a simple one-liner command:

Immediate

```
selection.offset(0,3).select
```

The result:

	A	B	C	D	E	F	G
1		123					
2		123					
3			123				
4			123				
5		123					
6				123			
7			123				
8			123				
9			123				
10			123				
11		123					
12		123					
13		123					
14			123				
15							

VBA Array

Suppose you needed to access a strange sequence of numbers, like 4,13,19,20,28,44,123. Perhaps these are rows you need to work on. You can get to them in a loop with this technique:

```
Sub AccessRows()
    For i = 0 To 6
        j = Array(4, 13, 19, 20, 28, 44, 123)(i)
        Rows(j).Font.Bold = True 'for example
    Next
End Sub
```

The statement Array(4,13,19,20,28,44,123) has 7 elements in it, numbered 0 through 6 (unless Option Base 1 is supplied at the top of the module). So the first element has a subscript of 0 and can be referenced by Array(4,13,19,20,28,44,123)(0), which would be a 4. The 123 is Array(4,13,19,20,28,44,123)(6). So, using i as a subscript, j takes on the successive values in the array list.

Here's another way to do the same thing. And since loops are so fast, you might simply prefer this way:

```
Sub AccessRows()
    For i = 4 To 123
        Select Case i
            Case 4, 13, 19, 20, 28, 44, 123
                Rows(i).Font.Bold = True
        End Select
    Next
End Sub
```

Split Bars in VBA

Did you know there are split bars in VBA? They're here:

Here's an excerpt from a very long routine and where the split bar was used to help align the If statement with the Else statement since there was a lot of nesting of statements:

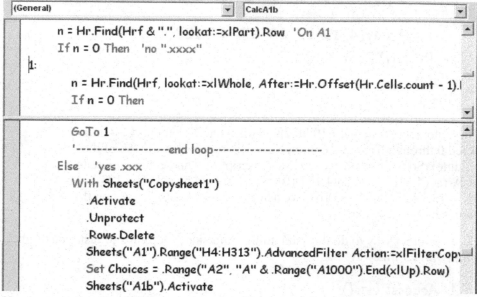

You can see that the split bar makes the alignment (since this author indents code to align the statements!) easier to see!

Where is the split bar originally? Here:

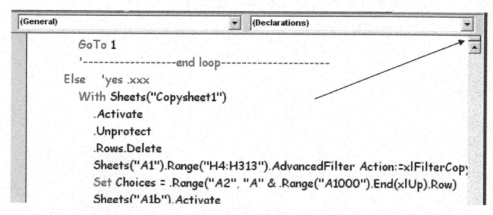

In VBA, did you know the Locals window is read/write?

The procedure SeeLocals was run and stopped at the End Sub:

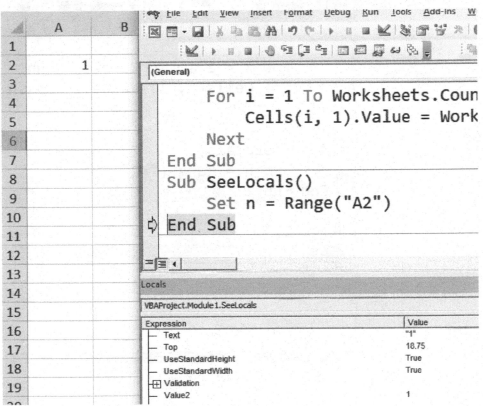

The locals window was brought up:

…and you can see that the 1 in cell A2 is shown at the bottom of the locals window in the first screenshot for this topic.

I then changed that 1 to a 25 *in the locals window:*

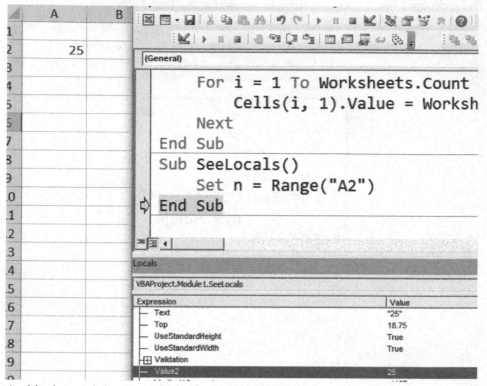

And it changed the 1 to a 25 in the worksheet!

Putting images in a Userform

You can do this with a simple copy/paste! Suppose you have this simple User-form with just an Image control on it:

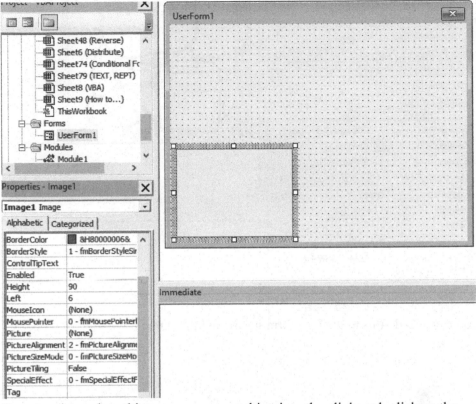

To get a picture into this, you can put anything into the clipboard, click on the Picture property, and paste! I used this picture:

Then I clicked the word Picture in the properties of the Image control and Ctrl/V:

You can also do this to the Userform itself – anything that has a Picture property.

Now I used this picture: and the result:

To remove the picture, select the picture property and use Ctrl/X!

Make your own tools in the toolbox!

You can right-click the control toolbox and select New Page (among others):

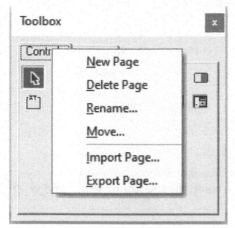

Then you can rename that page, etc. Here's my personal toolbox:

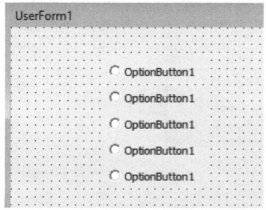

I have a set for option buttons, text boxes and just 3 text boxes. When I click on the option buttons one and drag it into the userform, I get something like this:

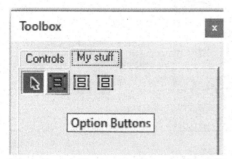

How did I get these? Once I have my new page, I create the buttons or option buttons or text boxes, etc. that I want to have easy access to (so I don't have to create them over and over each time) and I select them and drag them onto the toolbox!:

Suppose I wanted to be able to easily create 6 buttons like this:

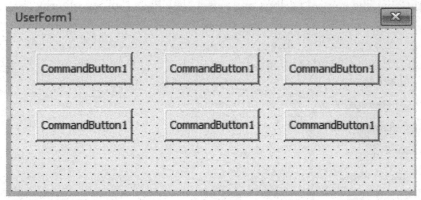

I would make these manually align them as I want, then select them all, and *drag* it onto the toolbox:

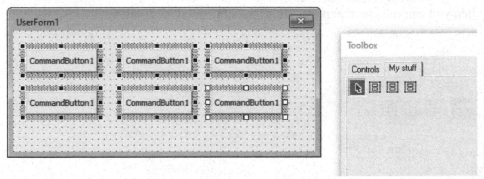

This would create a new button in the toolbox and then I right-click this button to customize it:

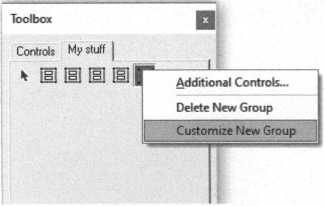

I give it a new name which shows when I hover over the control. As you can see, I can also load a picture onto the control so it's easier to identify.

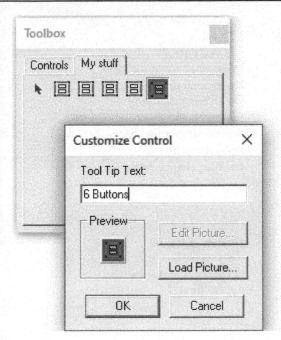

Index

Learn more from Bob Umlas with this book:

More Excel

OUTSIDE THE BOX

Unbelievable Excel Techniques
from Excel MVP Bob Umlas